W9-BYB-634

In Tune with God

The Art of Congregational Discernment

Sally Weaver Glick

Foreword by Marlene Kropf

Faith & Life Resources

A division of Mennonite Publishing Network

Scottdale, Pennsylvania
Waterloo, Ontario

Library of Congress Cataloging-in-Publication Data

Glick, Sally Weaver.
   In tune with God : the art of congregational discernment / by Sally Weaver Glick;
foreword by Marlene Kropf.
      p. cm.
   Includes bibliographical references.
   ISBN 0-8361-9284-2 (pbk. : alk. paper)
   1. Church management. 2. Discernment (Christian theology) 3. Decision
making—Religious aspects—Christianity. I. Title.
   BV652.9.G55 2004
   253—dc22

                                                          2004011927

IN TUNE WITH GOD: THE ART OF CONGREGATIONAL DISCERNMENT
by Sally Weaver Glick
Copyright © 2004 by Faith & Life Resources, Scottdale, PA 15683

International Standard Book Number: 0-8361-9284-2
Library of Congress Number 2004011927
Printed in the United States of America
Book and cover design by Merrill R. Miller
Cover photo by GoodShoot

10 09 08 07 06 05 04 10 9 8 7 6 5 4 3 2 1

To order or request information, please call 1-800-245-7894
Website: www.mph.org

For David and Beth,
as you learn to discern and join in with God's song

Table of Contents

Foreword

From her firsthand experience of the beauty and power of Mennonite singing, Sally Weaver Glick has opened the way for a fresh examination of the classic practice of spiritual discernment. *In Tune with God* shows discernment, practiced in the community of congregational life, as a lively interplay of God's unchanging melody and the endless variations of human response.

Weaving in and out of this song of discernment are three powerful refrains: about God, about community, and about ministry and mission. Not a one-note samba, the vision of discernment presented in this book borrows more from the intricacies of jazz improvisation or the multi-textured movement of a Bach chorale. The goal is an integration of the church's worship and work expressed in one rich, vibrant song of praise.

It's about God. This book begins at the appropriate starting place—with God. Rooted in prayer and worship, the practice of discernment requires a relationship with the living God. Because it is more about love and trust than about finding right answers, discernment can only grow in the context of spiritual habits that nurture a deepening relationship between God and the community of faith.

Even though discernment is always about God's song, Weaver Glick does not deny the demanding work believers are required to engage in as they seek to join God's song. She emphasizes that God's will is not something apart from ordinary human experience; rather, it is a creative collaboration of divine and human energy.

In the context of such a partnership, the author cautions that a prerequisite for good discernment may be to correct wrong images of God. False expectations of what God will do can undermine the work of discernment. Inadequate or distorted images of God can also limit the community's capacity to take responsibility for vision and action.

The work of discernment, therefore, cannot be picked up willy-nilly. Rather, it is the fruit of a loving, disciplined encounter with the God who longs to be made known and who desires human partnership in the healing of the world.

It's about community. Beyond a relationship with God, discernment requires a committed, loving relationship with other believers—something like the interaction of a chamber ensemble. Recognizing how counter-cultural this practice can be in our highly individualistic society—and even in the church—Weaver Glick acknowledges that congregations must nurture key practices for creating a climate of discernment. They must develop good listening skills, build trust, offer ample space for story-telling and sharing of experience, and encourage a playful, cooperative spirit even in the midst of struggle and disagreements.

The book is clear that the goal of spiritual discernment is not uniformity or unanimity but rather "unified diversity." Drawing upon a Quaker image, the author describes the outcome of corporate discernment as people remaining on different notes but blending them together as a pianist combines complementary notes in a chord.

To make good music, musicians need a conductor. *In Tune with God* underscores the important role of leadership even while expecting strong participation from each member of the congregation. With a ready repertoire of discernment strategies, leaders must exercise sound judgment as they choose appropriate processes, frame the issues as clearly as possible, carefully tend the use of power, and provide pastoral care for the congregation as a whole as well as for individuals throughout the process.

It's about ministry and mission. Healthy discernment practices make it possible for the church to join joyfully God's liberating song in the world. When believers are set free to flow with God's ever-moving Spirit, abundant creativity is released. Thus, in addition to deepening relationships with God and with one another, a church engaged in discernment becomes an active participant in the mending and healing of the world. Whether the church is making ethical decisions, deciding upon congregational practices, or engaging in vision development, all such discernment is for the sake of God's reign. Because it begins in love, discernment ends in love—expressed in worship and praise of the one true and living God.

It's a rich resource for congregations. No leader will be left wondering how to use this book. Beyond the useful real-life stories from congregations and the clear, accessible, biblically-grounded discussion of discernment, leaders will especially appreciate the practical tools provided: The whimsical "Dialogue for Two Fools" that introduces each chapter, the guidelines for actual discernment sessions (Appendix A), the leader's guide for a group study of *In Tune with God* (Appendix B), and a one-day retreat outline (Appendix C).

I take special pleasure in commending this book to the church, both because of its origin and because of the example it provides for other students of the Word. Inspired by courses she took at Associated Mennonite Biblical Seminary, Sally Weaver Glick pursued her study of discernment beyond the confines of the classroom. She integrated what she learned in her own congregational leadership, gleaned from others' experience, carefully crafted this fine book, and then generously offered it to God and to the church. As a seminary professor, I cannot imagine a more desirable outcome of study. May this book inspire the church to get in tune with God's song and sing it with great joy!

—*Marlene Kropf*
Congregational and Ministerial Leadership Team,
*   Mennonite Church USA*
Elkhart, Indiana

Acknowledgments

I would like to acknowledge and thank the many people who have contributed to this book as it has developed over the years.

I am grateful for the pastors who gave of their time to share with me about their congregation's experiences with discernment: Jim Amstutz and Dawn Yoder Harms, Akron Mennonite, Pennsylvania; Duane Beck and Nina Lanctot, Belmont Mennonite, Indiana; Daniel Schrock, Columbus Mennonite, Ohio; Florence Schloneger, First Mennonite of Beatrice, Nebraska; Vernon Rempel, First Mennonite of Denver, Colorado; Elaine Maust, Jubilee Mennonite, Mississippi; David Sutter, Kern Road Mennonite, Indiana; Donna Mast, Kingview Mennonite, Pennsylvania; Jane Roeschley, Mennonite Church of Normal, Illinois; Beth Ranck Yoder, Perkasie Mennonite, Pennsylvania; David Miller, University Mennonite, Pennsylvania; Sue Steiner, Waterloo North Mennonite, Ontario.

I appreciate the time and contributions of those who provided feedback on portions of this book at one stage or another of its development: Keith Harder, Rachel Miller Jacobs, Gayle Gerber Koontz, Karl Koop, Marlene Kropf, Brenda Lilliston and her 2004 Great Plains class on discernment, Brenda Hostetler Meyer, Mary Schertz, Dan Schrock, Marcus Smucker, Jeff Steckley, Carol Spicher Waggy, and Henry D. Weaver.

I am grateful for three congregations that have had a substantial role in shaping my understanding of and experience with congregational discernment: College Mennonite Church, Goshen, Indiana; Bloomington Monthly Meeting of the Society of Friends, Bloomington, Indiana; Assembly Mennonite Church, Goshen, Indiana. Thanks to the many fellow pilgrims there from whom I have learned, both when we have struggled to know how to discern together and when there has been healthy conflict and good discernment as we have journeyed together on Christ's Way.

Thanks also to the many friends whose words of wisdom and encouragement have kept me going, and especially to John, my spouse, friend, and fellow pilgrim. Without your support this book would never have come to be.

—*Sally Weaver Glick*
  Goshen, Indiana

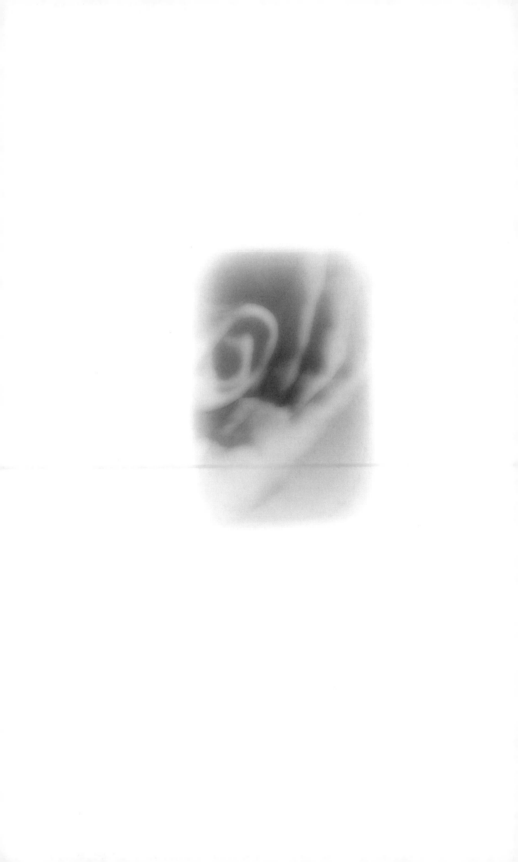

CHAPTER 1

Introduction: Singing God's Song

Discernment is the practice of tuning in to God's deepest desires for the world. It is the art of recognizing where God is already at work and of discovering what God is calling us to do or be in our own place and time. It is the discipline of aligning our decisions and actions with God's. *Congregational* discernment is the application of this practice to decisions made in and by the congregation.

In North America today, discernment has become something of a lost art. Our identity as Christian believers often has less impact on our decision-making practices than do influences from the secular world. We borrow and adapt the ways of community organizations, the business world, or the political arena. While we can learn useful skills from these sources, we also stand in danger of forgetting who and what we are. We stand in danger of forgetting the art of discernment.

Fortunately, there is also movement in the opposite direction. Across North America, there are individuals and congregations who value discernment. They are drawing on old practices and discovering new approaches that can transform congregational decision making. They have found approaches to goal setting and vision work that incorporate active listening for the guidance of the Holy Spirit. Many have encountered groups whose work with conflict strengthens and unites them instead of tearing them apart. They have experienced decisions being made in ways that respect the voices of all, not just the loudest, or the verbally gifted, or the powerful. They are glimpsing alternatives and wondering how to incorporate them into the way their congregations do business.

There are people like Laura who, five years ago, got involved in assisting court-ordered mediation cases in juvenile court. Then a nearby congregation wondered if she could do some mediation in a conflict they were dealing with. Her intervention went well, and soon another congregation was asking for her help. Laura's reputation spread and other congregations asked her to help in a variety of conflict situations. As her understanding of congregational conflict grew, she noticed that some congregations had developed ways of working with disagreements that treated conflict as opportunity rather than trouble. There are disagreements brewing in her own congregation over how the atonement should be understood, and she wonders what she can offer from her mediation training to help the congregation work with this issue.

There are people like Paul. A friend introduced Paul to the concept of a "clearness meeting" when Paul was facing a difficult choice between two jobs several years ago. This is an approach to decision making from the Quaker tradition where a small group gathers together to listen attentively to the individual and to the Holy Spirit. The friends that gathered around Paul brought a variety of experiences and backgrounds. Together they listened to him describe the choices and then began asking thoughtful and sometimes offbeat questions. They offered no solutions, but gave him plenty of space to listen for how the Spirit might be leading him. After meeting together a number of times, it became clear to Paul and to the group that one choice was the right one for him at that time. Paul is enthusiastic about this approach to decision making. He contrasts his experiences in the clearness meeting with the more parliamentarian approach of his large congregation. He is not sure how to translate his experiences with a small group into a congregational setting, but wonders what a clearness meeting approach could look like there.

There are congregations like First Christian Church of Middle Town, USA. It is not as large a congregation as Paul's, but its constitution and bylaws also rely on Robert's Rules of Order. The bylaws carefully list what constitutes a quorum, what percentage is needed for a majority vote, how proxy votes should be handled, and so on. There were good reasons for the congregation's original adoption of these rules. In an earlier decade, sloppiness in decision procedures led to a major conflict and then a split in the congregation. But some members are tired of the power plays and the behind-the-scenes maneuvers that still go on. "Our annual business meeting is a farce," one of them grumbles. "It's just a rubber-stamp for decisions the Board has already made." They wonder how to encourage decision making practices that are more consistent with being the body of Christ.

Peace Fellowship of Metro City, on the other hand, is a congregation where the members meet and discuss decisions monthly. All decisions are made by consensus. But some members here are also tired of the way things are done. "Process, process, process!" one says. "We're like gerbils running in a wheel. It takes so long and there are so many words. Are we really listening to each other and to God?" Members like the way everyone is involved, but decisions seem to take forever and sometimes it is hard to know if they have reached consensus or not. They wonder how to adapt their practices to help each other listen for God's leading while also making decisions in a more timely fashion.

And there are people like Janet, whose interest in congregational discernment grows out of her interest in spiritual formation work. Years ago, her pastor introduced her to spiritual disciplines. She began to practice some of these regularly—prayer, *lectio divina*, keeping a journal. She was especially intrigued by the idea of a spiritual director and began meeting once a month with a wise older woman. Through their work together, Janet felt she became more sensitive to ways God was at work in her life. Over time she became aware that God was inviting her to become a spiritual director for others. Over the past decade she has walked with many different people on their spiritual journeys. Recently her congregation has been wondering to what mission they are called. They are restless and feeling the need to clarify their congregational vision. Janet is wondering how the work she does with individuals might be adapted for the work of the congregation.

Pause for reflection

❧ *What has raised your interest in discernment?*

❧ *What resources or experiences of alternative ways of making decisions do you bring to this conversation?*

CONGREGATIONAL DISCERNMENT

Across North America, people and groups in different denominations have been exploring ways of making congregational decisions that transform the way their congregations go about business. They are drawing on insights from various backgrounds, including mediation work, consensus approaches, group dynamics studies, and spiritual discernment practices. They are rediscovering old methods of discernment and drawing on the experiences of groups such as the Quakers and the Ignatians. A flurry of books has emerged on the subject, coming from Methodists, Quakers, Catholics, Presbyterians, and others. While there are variations in what these writers propose, they all reflect the longing for a transformation in the way congregations do business. They share a vision for congregational discernment.

At the core of that vision is the recognition that our decision making is shaped by our identity as people of God and followers of Christ. In congregational discernment, we look to God. We try to discern where God is already at work, so that we can make decisions and take actions that are consistent with God's purposes and actions. We listen for where God wants to be at work, and where we are invited to join in. We draw on the best that we can bring in terms of our knowledge, our experiences, our wisdom and common sense, our intuition, and our imaginations. Prayerfully and attentively, we seek to discern the movement of the Spirit in our midst. Discerning this movement is not easy. Other voices compete for our attention. We need to listen with care and dedication to hear God's voice amid those others.

Picture this as music and movement. Think of God as singing us a song. In *The Magician's Nephew*, a story of the creation of a world, C. S. Lewis gives us a picture of his Christ-figure, the great lion Aslan, singing the world into existence. Picture God singing us such a song— a free-flowing song of creation and of steadfast love, of righteousness and peace. God yearns for the whole universe to join in singing this song, adding complex harmonies and improvising a joyous dance.

When we discern, we listen attentively in order to sort out what is God singing and what is mere static and noise. We let the song sing through us and shape us, so that we can join in harmoniously, responding to God's love and mercy. We watch for Jesus, the Lord of the Dance, so we can join him. And sometimes, as we watch and listen and join in, we sense a nod from the Divine Singer, inviting us to pick up on a particular phrase of the music and to play with it in our own unique way, moving and singing.

Discerning God's song takes place on many different levels. Individuals discern invitations along their journey of faith, often with the help of others. Church groups of all sizes, from committees and small groups up through church institutions and denominational bodies, listen for God's song. The focus of this book, however, is squarely on the congregation and the decisions we make together as members of a congregation. Whether we come from a denomination that is hierarchically or congregationally structured, there are always decisions to be made at the congregational level. How this works varies by denomination, but the core remains the same. In congregational discernment, we come together as a particular gathering of the people of God, joining with our sisters and brothers to discern God's song, so that our decisions and actions will be in tune with God.

TELLING OUR STORIES

In any discernment process, each of us brings our past with us. The same is true for this discussion of congregational discernment. We all come with stories, the experiences that have shaped our understanding of what discernment is and what it might be. I would like to share with you some of my stories, to give you a glimpse of the way my past has nurtured my conviction that congregational discernment is both possible and a vital part of what it means to be the people of God.

My background is Mennonite. Mennonites are part of the free-church tradition. While we do have regional conferences and national denominations that come to agreements together, most decisions are congregationally based. Many congregations make their decisions by some mixture of discussion and voting, while other congregations use consensus. The large Mennonite congregation in which I grew up relied on Roberts' Rules of Order and voting for formal decisions, plus a lot of informal discussion outside business meetings.

As a college student, I experienced another approach. I joined a young, energetic Mennonite congregation that looked to its Anabaptist roots to shape its decision making procedures. We worked with a consensus model. This worked fairly well for the first several years. Then came a more challenging decision. At that time we had no building, worshipping instead in three different Sunday morning gatherings, one on the college campus, one in a doctor's lobby, and one in a downtown dance studio. While we all met together every seventh Sunday in a rented location, we had no place of our own. For some, this was an ideal approach, requiring little overhead or upkeep, freeing time and money for ministries. For others, it was a disadvantage to have no home base, no space to center us and to reach out from.

Then a near-by building came up for sale—not a church, but a factory for sewing cheerleading uniforms. Some members gifted with vision and carpentry skills saw ways that it could be renovated to suit our needs. The discernment process began, an experience that left me with a deep and abiding sense that congregational discernment is possible. True, it took longer than any of us had expected. There were more members' meetings in the basement of the college library than I care to recall. Some, convinced that buying a building was the right thing to do and that the location of this one was ideal, were on pins and needles, afraid the opportunity would be gone before we would reach a conclusion. Still, they took the time to listen deeply to those who felt buying the building would be the wrong decision, weighing their reasons carefully.

Our discussions were sometimes heated and full of emotion, but through it all people were doing their best to hear each other's points of view and to be attentive to God's leading. We worked together until all of us were either convinced that buying the building was the right move or were willing to let the congregation go ahead, despite reservations. More than 25 years later that building, renovated and later remodeled and expanded, continues as home for the congregation. While some of the concerns raised during the discernment have come true, so too have the hopes and dreams. More of the congregational budget is indeed spent internally on maintenance, but the building houses two congregations and a daycare center, and God is at work there.

Other experiences also shape my understanding of congregational discernment. During our graduate school years, my husband and I became Sojourning Members of a Society of Friends' Meeting. We attended the weekly silent worship and participated in the monthly meeting for business. We also served on several clearness committees over the years. In one, we were invited to help a young pregnant student decide whether to give up her child for adoption. In another, we used fairly structured guidelines to provide pre-marital counseling for an engaged couple. In yet another, we met weekly for months, providing a place of listening and prayer for a struggling married couple. We called together our own clearness committee to help us discern where we should go after graduation. I valued those times of gathered silence, actively listening for the wind of the Spirit. From the Friends I learned much about reading the sense of the meeting and about the importance of allowing space and silence for active listening.

Back among Mennonites, I have been in various leadership roles in my congregation as we have worked with some complex decisions over the past fifteen years. We decided to expand and renovate our building, we made the move from having only lay leadership to having a pastoral team, and we wrestled with strongly contrasting opinions about how to respond to gays and lesbians seeking membership. Most of these decisions were made through consensus. This continues to be an approach I value, though I have also become more aware of its difficulties, especially when feelings run strong. Despite the best of intentions, we do not always hear each other or God. I have also become more aware of the complexities that result when one congregation's discernment is at odds with other congregations it relates to, and when congregations have different understandings of how congregational discernment should be done.

For part of the time that I was involved in these on-the-ground, practical experiences, I was also studying at Associated Mennonite Biblical Seminaries. While the focus of my Master of Divinity work was in biblical studies, discernment was a theme I kept returning to, not only in my church and ministry classes, but also in my theological and biblical studies. I was able to delve into some of the many recent writings on discernment and to begin putting into words an Anabaptist-Mennonite perspective on congregational discernment. This book grows out of the seeds sown there.

In Mennonite circles these days, there is much talk of transformation. The newly formed Mennonite Church USA is developing its identity and establishing ways of doing things that reflect the past but are not bound by it. It is an opportune time to examine our congregational and denominational decision making practices. Discernment is a crucial element in being the missional church we have said we want to be. Mennonite churches and individuals are among the many who are exploring ways of grounding decision making in discernment. This book invites us all to enter the conversation. While I claim as my own an Anabaptist-Mennonite framework, I have learned much from writers coming from other traditions. I trust that this book will be equally useful to the Mennonite conversation and to congregations and individuals who come from other perspectives.

Pause for reflection

What stories of congregational discernment do you carry?

What elements of them give you hope? What elements raise cautions or concerns? What do you wonder about?

USING THIS BOOK

This book is for all those people who lie awake at night thinking about what might have improved that church business meeting. It is for those who are looking for ways to get their congregation thinking about discernment. It is for those who bring insights and skills that enhance discernment and who are wondering how to use them in the congregational setting. It is for those groups and congregations who want to renew and transform the way they do business together. It is for you, with whatever particular mix of curiosity and hope you bring.

Too often we do our congregational decision making from habit, based on the way we have always done it or on models we are familiar with from other settings. This book is an invitation for a more attentive look at what we do and why. Its fundamental premise is that congregational discernment is a corporate spiritual discipline. Both the decisions we make and the way we come to those decisions should be deeply shaped by our identity as people of God and followers of Christ.

Because congregational discernment is a corporate spiritual discipline, this book is designed for corporate discussion. Many books on discernment are aimed at those leading a discernment process. While it is indeed important that leaders be aware of all that discernment can be, it is equally important that the congregation as a whole develop a common understanding of what we are trying to do in our congregational discernment. I don't go as far as some in the Ignatian tradition, who hold that true communal discernment only happens when all the individuals in that community are proficient in individual spiritual discernment. A critical mass of praying, discerning individuals is important, but our congregations always include people at many different levels of spiritual maturity. Just as we worship with this reality, so too we do our congregational discernment with the same reality. Still, both our worship and our discernment can be enhanced as we learn more about them together.

This is not primarily a how-to book, although I have gathered specific suggestions and practices from many sources; those interested can turn to Appendix A for these helpful ideas. The book as a whole, however, is a primer—a book that covers the basic foundations of a subject. I invite you to enter a conversation reviewing these foundations, examining our assumptions, bringing our diverse experiences and insights together, listening for the guidance of the Holy Spirit. In short, I invite you to enter into discernment about how you might deepen your own congregation's discernment and decision making.

This book covers basic areas that shape our understanding of congregational discernment and how we can best go about it. Chapter 2 explores what congregational discernment is and is not, and reviews New Testament passages dealing with congregational decision making for the insights they can give us today. Chapter 3 delves into the foundation for all our discernment—our relationship with God. We discern so that we can respond faithfully to God's love for us, joining in God's song. Therefore it is appropriate to examine the images of God that we carry, and to be aware of the need for occasional spring-cleaning in strengthening that relationship. The chapter also looks at God's self-revelation in Scripture as the three-fold unity of Creator, Christ, and Spirit, and the implications this love-spilling-over, vulnerable, invitational character of God has for our approach to discernment.

Appropriate worship involves responding to God's love with praise in word and action. Chapter 4 looks at the role of discernment for this response to God and helps us explore the key concept of God's will. "God's will" is a phrase that carries a lot of weight. The chapter helps us examine our assumptions and invites us to broaden our understanding of the phrase through a look at the biblical usage of "God's will." With Chapter 5, our focus turns to the people of God, and the new, diverse community we are in Christ. It discusses the God-given gifts of diversity and disagreement and encourages us to develop habits of healthy conflict.

Chapter 6 goes over the basic framework for creative discernment and describes several phases of the process, each with its own distinct tasks. Having a clear idea of some of these basic landmarks can help us better understand where we are in the midst of our discernment. It also offers a look at the roles of the congregation and of leadership in the process of discernment. Chapter 7 looks at the role the Bible plays in our discernment. Rather than a source of ammunition to be hurled at one another, the Bible is formational for the development of Christian identity and imagination, contributes to our encounter with the living Word, and encourages us as we attempt to embody faithfully the Christian Way. The chapter suggests ways we can grow as wise readers, taking the voice of Scripture seriously in our discernment conversation. Chapter 8 examines some of the complications and barriers we may encounter and shares stories of how several Mennonite congregations are incorporating discernment in their decision making. It also opens the conversation about the next steps to be taken in your own congregation.

Throughout these chapters you will find pauses for reflection. I invite you to take time out from your reading to ponder these questions. You may want to spend time writing your responses or other ideas in a journal. One teacher who relies heavily on the journal as a teaching tool notes that we are often so intent on our reading that we don't allow our own ideas and responses to flourish. We think we are thinking, but in reality all we have is a tight little bud of a thought. We need to provide space and time for it to open into full bloom. One solution to this is to keep a journal, pausing as you read to jot down your reflections and questions.

We read and ponder individually, but my hope is that you will then gather with others for discussion, bringing the flowers from your reading and reflection together to create a unique bouquet. This book is intended to initiate discussion and interactions in small group settings—an adult Sunday school class, an Elder Board, a gathering of interested individuals, a congregation. For this reason, Appendix B has suggestions for group sessions in connection with each chapter. These suggestions include questions for discussion and invitations to try one or more of the practices that can enhance our congregational discernment. It is difficult for one person, on his or her own, to transform the way we do church business. Change comes as we talk, reflect, and pray together, and as we envision new ways of doing things.

Each of the following chapters begins with a dialogue between two Fools for Christ. Holy fools have long been part of the Christian tradition. They are those whose deep but light-hearted relationship with God allows them to approach a difficult topic with a twist of humor and insight that can help the rest of us see things in a new light. They resonate with Paul's words to the Corinthians: "If you think that you are wise in this age, you should become fools so that you may become wise" (1 Corinthians 3:18). Holy fools are not afraid to ask the foolish questions and to explore new avenues of understanding.

The dialogues by the two Fools in this book introduce key concepts of the chapter in a light-hearted way. My hope is that they can free us to ask our own "foolish" questions, to venture into areas that we wonder about, and to explore them together. These dialogues can also be presented in the small group setting to review the chapter and initiate discussion. In the congregational setting they can be used as a skit along with a sermon or a presentation on the chapter's topic. Many of them have been used and enjoyed in this way in my own congregation. We have invited different people to take on the role of the Fools each time and have been surprised and delighted by the way people live into the opportunity of asking foolish questions.

Good discernment can and does happen. Congregations can and have transformed their ways of doing business together. It does not happen overnight. There is no magic wand, no set of techniques that always works, no facilitator who always brings resolution, no experienced congregation that always manages to discern joyfully and fruitfully. But as we journey together there will be moments of vision and awareness of God's work in the world, moments when we know who we are and to what we are called. When true discernment happens, creativity is released, energy is freed for tackling problems together, and relationships with God and one another are strengthened. My prayer is that through your work with this book your congregation may also continue to open itself to the gift of discernment.

Discernment

Notes: When done as reader's theater, the two fools wear jester's hats and something to indicate their "fool" status—a patchwork vest, a bright tie or colorful, mismatched clothing. For each dialogue, one of them carries a kit sack (a large, lumpy drawstring bag such as a laundry sack would work well). Some of the dialogues will involve props from this sack; at other times it will simply be there. Additional readers will be needed for some of the dialogues. You may want to inform the congregation or group that the fools' names are meaningful: "Theophilus" means "God-lover" in Latin while "Amadeus" is "God-lover" in Greek.

Props: Dictionary, copy of *In Tune with God*

T: Hi! I'm Theophilus.

A: and I'm Amadeus.

T: We're pilgrims on a journey.

A: Two fools for Christ who wander the world,

T: trying to put into words what can't be put into words,

A: trying to understand mystery and paradox and talk about them with people like you.

T: So, what are we talking about today, Amadeus?

A: The word for today, Theophilus, is . . . *discernment*.

T: All right! Discernment! (*Pause*) Ummm—discernment? What's that when it's at home?

A: Discernment?

T: Yeah, discernment.

A: Well, you know . . . It's discernment.

T: You don't know either, do you?

A: Well, I know it's something churches do. And it's got a nice swing to it—dis-*cern*-ment (*emphasizing second syllable and illustrating the swing of it with a broad arm sweep to the side*).

T: Okay, but we're supposed to be helping these people do some thinking and talking about discernment. You can't just stand there and swing.

A: Dis-*cern*-ment.

T: Amadeus?

A: Um, right. Discernment. Okay, well, how about a dictionary? Have you got a dictionary on you?

T: Let me look . . . (*checks kit sack*). Well, lookee here! I just happen to have one.

A: So, what's it say?

T: Hang on, hang on. Let's see . . . discernment, discernible, okay, it's under discern:
- to detect or perceive with the eyes or intellect;
- to perceive the distinctions of, to discriminate.

A: To discriminate?! I thought that was bad.

T: No, they don't mean discriminate like in prejudice. It's the other meaning. Just a sec . . . (*turns page*). Here it is—discriminating:
- able to recognize or draw fine distinctions;
- showing careful judgment or fine taste.

A: Okay, so discernment is about sorting things out, seeing those fine distinctions.

T: Hey, it's like that Sesame Street song: "One of these things just doesn't belong here, three of these things are kinda the same, one of these things is not like the others, can you tell which one by the something something game?"

A: Well, maybe. But what does that have to do with the church?

T: Hmm, it doesn't sound quite like the way the word gets used around here, does it?

A: You don't by any chance have a church lingo dictionary in that bag, do you?

T: (*Checks*) No, I'm afraid not.

A: Well, maybe we can figure it out some other way. (*Both ponder, with Amadeus muttering dis-cern-ment under his breath and making swinging motion with his arm again.)*

T: Will you cut that out?

A: (*Getting idea*) Hey, isn't this congregation using a book about discernment? Maybe that would help.

T: Good idea! (*Turns to pastor/Sunday school teacher/congregational leader*) Do you have a copy we could borrow? (*Receives* In Tune with God *and holds it unopened*) Thanks! Okay, Amadeus, so what do we want to know?

A: Well, what is discernment?

T: Okay. (*Addresses book*) What is discernment? (*Sets book on table or podium, holding book upright between palms, then allows it to fall open where it will and, carefully gazing up at ceiling, puts forefinger on a spot.*) What does it say?

A: (*Leaning in to read*) "Discernment is *not* just a fancy word for decision making." Hmm, what do you think, Theophilus?

T: Well, sometimes we talk as though that's what it is.

A: Yeah, "The elders discerned that we need new carpet in the worship space."

T: But, you know, I think maybe the book is right. It *should* be more than that.

A: Try again.

T: Okay, let's see. (*Same routine*) There.

A: (*Reading*) "Discernment is *not* just finding the lowest common denominator."

T: Well, of course not. That would hardly be discriminating, would it?

A: Maybe we can find out more (*Motions for T to do it again, which he does. Reads*). "Discernment is *not* the same thing as consensus."

T: Whoa! Isn't this treading on holy ground? At least some churches seem to think consensus is sacred.

A: I'm getting confused. What *is* discernment? Let me see that. (*Takes the book and begins looking.*) Here it is, right at the beginning. "Discernment is the practice of tuning in to God's deepest desires for the world. It is the art of recognizing where God is already at work and of discovering what God is calling us to in our own time and place. It is the discipline of aligning our decisions and actions with God's." (*A begins softly saying "dis-cern-ment" and sweeping right arm to the side on* cern.)

T: Yes, but what does all that mean? Aligning decisions and so forth?

A: Dis-*cern*-ment. (*Right arm sweep on* cern *moves into 1-2-3 conducting motion*)

T: Amadeus!

A: Well, Theophilus, maybe it's a little like listening for a song. (*Continues "conducting"*)

T: A song?

A: Yeah, a song. (*Stops*) What if God were singing us a song? Then discernment would be us listening for that song.

T: Hmmm—you mean, like, figuring out what is in tune with the song? And sorting that out from all the noise or static?

A: Yeah. (*Gets another idea*) And maybe sometimes God is like a jazz musician.

T: A jazz musician?

A: Yeah. See, God doesn't want to be a solo singer. God wants us to join in.

T: But what does that have to do with jazz?

A: Well, we better be listening, because the Holy Spirit might just invite us to take off on an improvised riff, jamming and having a great time living out all that peace, and justice, and righteousness that God is singing about.

T: You know, Amadeus, I think maybe I'm beginning to get an idea of what discernment is. But I'm still feeling pretty confused.

A: Well, we're just at the beginning of our study. There'll be more to learn next week.

T: Guess you're right. So we'll see you folks again later.

A: And remember—dis-*cern*-ment. It's got swing!

CHAPTER 2

Determine What Is Best

SPOTTING THE HERON

I walk regularly with two friends. Nearly every morning we go a couple of miles along a nearby canal, walking, and talking, and practicing our novice bird-watching skills. Great blue herons stake out this stretch of the canal. We often see one or two a morning, each one a solitary sentry at the water's edge, motionless but alert, long bill poised to snatch its breakfast from the shallows. A glimpse of one of these sentinels always causes us to break off our conversation as one of us points with mild triumph, quietly exclaiming, "There's the heron."

One recent winter morning we began walking just before dawn. I was in the midst of working on this chapter and as we walked along the path we discussed how we use "discern" and "discernment" in ordinary speech. "Use one in a sentence," I said to the other two, "something that doesn't have anything to do with congregational discernment."

They thought for a while and then one friend offered, "It was difficult to discern the path in the dark woods." Just then I spotted a heron a little ahead of us and on the other side of the canal. I interrupted our discussion to point it out: "There's the heron." The others peered through the dim light. One shook her head. "I think it's just a branch. Can't you see the trunk in the water?" A recent ice storm had added downed trees and branches to our familiar walk and, as we drew nearer, I had to agree. There was the tree in the water and that stick-like figure I had thought was a heron was just a branch jutting up. The brush behind it had confused me. Or had it?

As we got still closer and saw it from yet another angle, the image leapt into new clarity. Yes, there was the trunk in the water, and there was the brush that made it difficult to distinguish exactly what we were seeing. But our new angle revealed that there was also a heron perched there, its white face and black crest standing out clearly in the increasing light. By now it had also spotted us and it lumbered into flight, swooping on its wide wings to some other less populated stretch of water.

"Discern" and "discernment" are not the most common words in the English language, but we do have some sense of what they mean. They have to do with perceiving fine distinctions, distinguishing one thing from another. In the dim morning light, it was difficult to discern what was stick and what was heron. Unintentionally, we entered a process of discernment, trying to see more clearly as we peered and came closer. Finally, with a sense of discovery and delight, we came to a conclusion, a moment of discernment, when we could tell with certainty what was tree branch, what was brush, and what was heron.

In this case of the heron, it was a simple matter of visual discernment. We sorted out what we were seeing, distinguishing stick from bird. When we use "discern" in ordinary usage, we are often referring to some similar use of our senses—using our sight, or touch, or hearing to distinguish one thing from another. At other times it is our specialized knowledge that allows us to make distinctions. The art historian is able to discern the touch of a master's hand in the sure brush strokes on a particular painting. The trained lab technician peering through the microscope is able to discern healthy cells from diseased ones. While my walking companions and I are able to distinguish heron from stick, we are often stumped by the different birdcalls we hear. Some day perhaps we will invite an experienced bird-watcher to walk with us and share her knowledge of the distinguishing details.

Another familiar use comes when we talk about people who show good discernment. We are not referring to their heron-spotting abilities, or even their specialized knowledge. We mean that they make good choices, good decisions. They distinguish a wise course of action from a foolish one. They have good taste. They pick out life-giving friends from those who would lead them astray. Someone with poor discernment, on the other hand, is likely to make a mess of things, consistently making wrong decisions, unable to spot a good choice in the camouflage of bad ones.

Pause for reflection

❦ Congregational discernment is not a commonly used phrase, either inside or outside the church. Does your congregation use it? How?

❦ What do you think of when you hear it? What memories or images or associations come to mind for you, if any?

A CORPORATE SPIRITUAL DISCIPLINE

When I invite you to reflect on what "congregational discernment" means to you, different ideas may spring to mind. Some people think primarily of interpretation of Scripture. For others, the first thing to come to mind will be vision-work, finding new directions for the church and its ministry. Mennonites give discernment of ethical issues high priority. Some people only use "discernment" to refer to a particular type of decision—choosing leadership, perhaps, or deciding between several possible courses of action. No single one of these strands adequately encompasses the fullness of congregational discernment; all are important. With each, we want to be listening for God's song.

Dictionary definitions of "discern" and "discernment" emphasize the use of the senses and intellect in making fine distinctions, and in distinguishing one thing from another. They focus on the here and now—on physical reality. When we use "discernment" in the religious sense, we broaden our framework. Just as with the common usage, spiritual discernment calls for making fine distinctions and wise choices. But we do not limit our awareness of distinctions to the physical world. Instead, we understand those distinctions to be held by a wider, deeper reality. We open ourselves to God, being attentive to God's presence. We attempt to discern God's song, making choices that are consistent with who God is and what God is doing in the world.

Discernment is not just a fancy word for decision making.

Discernment and decision making are closely related, but they are not the same thing. Decisions in many different settings are made without any concern for who God is or what God desires. Discernment is not just business-as-usual, using the same factors and framework as any other organization. With discernment, our decision making is shaped by our identity as people of God and followers of Christ.

Congregational discernment is a corporate spiritual discipline. It is a creative, informed, attentive, and interactive practice of the church, led by the Holy Spirit. It involves both *movement*, as we peer and draw nearer and perceive new angles, and *moment*, when our efforts crystallize into new clarity. This clarity then draws us into decision and action. Like other corporate spiritual disciplines such as gathered worship, congregational discernment is a practice that can deepen our relationship with God and help us grow into the fullness of Christ, both as individuals and as a congregation. Prayer, scripture meditation, fasting, attentive silence, song, hospitality, and other such spiritual disciplines feed into and nourish it.

For some people, congregational discernment automatically translates as consensus. Discernment is *not* the same thing as consensus. Consensus is one particular method of decision making. It is a good method, and the process used to reach consensus has much to contribute to discernment. But it is not in and of itself the same as congregational discernment. Many non-church groups use a consensus approach to decision making, but have no interest in listening for God's song. Equally, other methods of congregational decision making may not reach a consensus, but still find ways to be attentive to God's purposes and actions in the world.

Congregations make decisions in many ways. There are formal methods, such as voting or the use of consensus. Decisions may also be made by informal discussion, by an authorized leader or committee making a decision on behalf of the whole, and even by default, when a decision results from no decision being made. All of these methods can be used without any concern for discernment of God's will. On the other hand, except for decisions by default, discernment can be a vital part of any method. If we are prayerfully attentive to God, to each other, and to God's purposes and actions in the world, opening ourselves to God's reality, a number of different decision making methods can be compatible with discernment.

Pause for reflection

❧ *What decision making methods does your congregation use?*

❧ *How do prayer, scriptural meditation, silence, and other scriptural disciplines nourish your method?*

❧ *Does your congregation see its gatherings for decision making as a corporate spiritual discipline? If not, how does it understand them?*

THREE BIBLICAL VOICES ON DISCERNMENT

Congregational discernment is a spiritual discipline. As with any spiritual discipline, it is something that any believer can participate in, but it is also something that can be practiced more fruitfully with care and attention. Certain practices and attitudes help us toward greater maturity, both as individuals and as congregations. To better understand the spiritual discipline of congregational discernment, it is appropriate to begin by seeing what we can learn from the church's book, the Bible.

Stories from Acts: A Descriptive Voice

Acts gives us several stories of times when the young church engaged in discernment and decision making. These stories are *descriptive* rather than *prescriptive*—Luke is describing events, not laying down rules for all times and places. His focus is on telling the story of the church's growth, not on writing a how-to manual for congregational discernment. We cannot turn to the stories for a complete picture of how we are to go about our discernment. But we can get some glimpses of what discernment involved for the early church, which may give us some clues for our understanding of congregational discernment today.

On two occasions, the young church needed to choose leaders. The first happened before Pentecost, when 120 believers were gathered together, praying and waiting. With Judas' death, they had a leadership slot to fill. The gathering proposed two names from among those who had followed Jesus, and then they prayed for guidance. They cast lots, and Matthias was added to the eleven apostles (Acts 1:15–26).

Later, after Pentecost, when their numbers were increasing dramatically, the young church ran into more leadership problems. The young group included both Jews and Greeks, and some began complaining that the Greek widows weren't getting their fair share of the daily distribution of bread. The apostles called together the whole community of disciples, and together they selected seven men of good standing who could oversee this distribution. Once chosen, these men stood before the apostles, who prayed and laid hands on them (Acts 6:1–6).

At other times, the church looked for direction in ministry. The leaders of the church in Antioch were worshipping God and fasting when they heard the Holy Spirit calling on them to send Barnabas and Saul on a mission trip. After more fasting and prayer they commissioned the two and sent them off (Acts 13:1–3).

Then there was the hot topic of the day, the question of whether or not Gentile believers would need to be circumcised, an issue that created "no small dissension and debate." Questions first came up after Peter baptized Cornelius, a devout Gentile and a centurion of the Italian Cohort. When Peter visited the church in Jerusalem, there were questions and criticisms. How could he eat with Gentiles? How could he baptize someone who had not first been circumcised? Peter responded with his story—the vision of being offered unclean meat and refusing, only to be told that, "What God has cleansed you must not call common," and then the invitation to speak with Cornelius, and the pouring out of the gift of the Holy Spirit on the unbaptized household. How could he *not* eat with Gentiles? How could he *not* respond with baptism when the household had received the same gift of the Spirit that the disciples had received? Persuaded by his words and the corroboration of the circumcised believers who had been with him, the Jerusalem church accepted his action (Acts 10:1—11:18).

But that still left the broader issue of circumcision. Questions continued to fly about how Gentiles were to be included in the new church. Later the discussion got particularly heated in Antioch, and Paul and Barnabas traveled to Jerusalem to consult with the apostles and the elders there. Again there was much debate. The turning point came as Peter told again of the way the Holy Spirit had come to Cornelius' household. The whole assembly listened in attentive silence, and then Paul and Barnabas told of their own experiences among believing Gentiles. James summarized their stories and related these experiences to the words of the prophets concerning Gentiles who seek the Lord. He proposed a resolution: the church would not expect Gentile believers to be circumcised, but they should abstain from idolatry, fornication, and blood. The apostles and elders, with the consent of the whole church, decided to send several men to Antioch, bearing a letter with the word that "it has seemed good to the Holy Spirit and to us" to impose no further burden than these few specific restrictions (Acts 15:1–29).

In these descriptive stories of the early church, we see congregations of believers making decisions. They fill leadership roles, engage in problem solving, develop mission work, and respond to controversy and conflict. Each situation involves a group gathering to discern together. Prayer and worship are common threads, but there is no set method of decision making. Each occasion is unique.

Pause for reflection

❧ *What does Luke tell us in each story of congregational discernment? What is the decision about? Who makes it? What methods are used?*

❧ *What are some of the elements of worship and discernment Luke describes?*

The Rule of Paul: A Prescriptive Voice

The stories in Acts describe certain events in the early church, but they do not propose rules or guidelines. Other biblical passages do give guidelines—the Ten Commandments and the Sermon on the Mount are two obvious examples. While there are no neatly laid out "Rules for Congregational Discernment," we do have some *prescriptive* passages written for young congregations who were trying to figure out details of their life together. One such passage is known as "the Rule of Paul." The congregation in Corinth wrote to Paul, their founder, with many questions. In response to their questions about spiritual gifts, Paul has some directions about how those gifts are to be used in orderly worship.

What should be done then, my friends? When you come together, each one has a hymn, a lesson, a revelation, a tongue or an interpretation. Let all things be done for building up. If anyone speaks in a tongue, let there be only two or at most three, and each in turn; and let one interpret. But if there is no one to interpret, let them be silent in church and speak to themselves and to God. Let two or three prophets speak, and let the others weigh what is said. If a revelation is made to someone else sitting nearby, let the first person be silent. For you can all prophesy one by one, so that all may learn and all be encouraged. And the spirits of prophets are subject to the prophets, for God is a God not of disorder but of peace (1 Corinthians 14:26–33).

The link between congregational discernment and this "Rule of Paul" may not be immediately apparent, because many churches understand gatherings for worship and gatherings for decision making as two very different things. This was not the case in the early church. As we saw in the stories from Acts, worship and discernment were closely connected. In this case, Paul is concerned that the Corinthians' time together be peaceful and constructive, building them up as faithful disciples. Discernment is part of this. Prophecies are to be weighed and tested in the gathered congregation. A similar message appears in 1 John 4:1 ("Beloved, do not believe every spirit, but test the spirits to see whether they are from God . . .") and 1 Thessalonians 5:20–22 ("Do not despise the words of prophets, but test everything; hold fast to what is good; abstain from every form of evil").

Pause for reflection

*❧ What does Paul recommend about worship
in this passage?*

*❧ Which of these recommendations about worship relate
to discernment?*

Paul's Letter to the Philippians: A Prayerful Voice

The first chapter of Paul's letter to the Philippians includes a prayer for that community (Philippians 1:9–11). It speaks of discernment, but it is neither a descriptive nor a prescriptive passage. It is a prayer, a vision for how things might be, a hope for what the church in Philippi might yet become. In a succinct form it expresses many themes that Paul develops more fully elsewhere, related to community life and our work of discernment together. To appreciate the fullness of this prayer, it can be helpful to unfold it slowly, taking time with each phrase.

And this is my prayer, that your love may overflow more and more . . .

Paul's letter is addressed to the saints in Philippi, a church which he began and which was near and dear to his heart. He was "constantly praying with joy in every one of my prayers for all of you" (Philippians 1:4). When we sit and read our Bibles quietly at home, it can be hard to remember that Paul was not writing to scattered individuals, but to a congregation. His prayer is for the Philippian church as a whole, and his beginning point is abundant love, love that overflows more and more. In this we can hear again Jesus' commandment: "Love one another," or his "By this shall all know that you are my disciples—if you have love one for another."

Jesus and Paul do not begin with power, or purity, or perfection. They do not begin with rules and propositions, but with relationship. Their beginning point is love, the love that God has for the world, the love that Jesus modeled, the love that gives itself so that others might also love and live. Jesus named it as the greatest commandment: "The first is, 'Hear, O Israel: the Lord our God, the Lord is one; you shall love the Lord your God with all your heart, and with all your soul, and with all your mind, and with all your strength.' The second is this, 'You shall love your neighbor as yourself'" (Mark 12:29–31). Paul sounds this same call to love over and over again in his prayers and teachings—see 1 Thessalonians 3:12–13, Galatians 5:13–14, Romans 12:9–10, Ephesians 3:17–19 and 5:1–2, and especially his great hymn to love, 1 Corinthians 13. Our congregational discernment is rooted and grounded in love.

. . . *with knowledge and full insight* . . .

In 1 Corinthians 12 Paul goes into detail about the gifts that the Holy Spirit gives the church for the common good, which include the utterance of wisdom, the utterance of knowledge, and the discernment of spirits. The Spirit gives the community what is needed for the work of ministry and for building up the body of Christ. These gifts come to individuals, but they are in service of the whole community. No one person has all the knowledge and insight needed, but by combining our gifts we can discern together.

. . . *to help you determine what is best* . . .

The Greek word *dokimazo*, here translated as *determine*, is also at times translated as *approve*, or *discern*, or *test*. It comes from the Greek word for testing a substance such as a metal, to see whether it is genuine. It can also refer to something that has passed such an examination and been approved or found worthy. It can be either the testing or the result: "This is the good stuff." Paul's prayer is that the community will be able to examine their lives and the world around them and that they will know what passes the test, what is best. *Dokimazo* appears in other familiar passages: Paul encourages the Romans to *dokimazo* the "will of God— what is good and acceptable and perfect" (Romans 12:2), and the Ephesians to *dokimazo* "what is pleasing to the Lord," the fruit of the light found in all that is "good and right and true" (Ephesians 5:9–10). When we are grounded in love, with the gifts of the Spirit, we will discern "the good stuff."

. . . so that in the day of Christ you may be pure and blameless . . .

Just a few verses earlier, Paul writes, "I am confident of this, that the one who began a good work among you will bring it to completion by the day of Jesus Christ" (Philippians 1:6). The congregation is a "work-in-progress." The Holy Spirit has begun to transform their lives, both as individuals and as a congregation, but this change is not yet complete. They are the saints in Philippi, but they have not yet arrived at all they shall become. Paul is looking ahead to the day when Christ will return and all will be judged. Paul's prayer is that the Philippians will be able to recognize what is pleasing to God and to live this out in their lives, so that when judged they will not be found wanting.

Paul knows the church has not yet reached maturity—his letters are written to churches struggling with problems of many kinds, and he himself was often in the midst of disagreements and wrangling. Still, he holds out the vision of what we are aiming for: love and discernment that leads to behavior that is ever more Christ-like.

. . . having produced the harvest of righteousness that comes through Jesus Christ . . .

Our modern North American ears have a hard time with "righteousness." We can hardly hear it as anything but *self*-righteousness, a smug self-satisfied piety. This is a far cry from the harvest of righteousness that comes through Jesus Christ! Righteousness is better understood as right relationship, with God and with others. Think of the parable of the Day of Judgment in Matthew 25, where the Son of Man separates the righteous—those who have done what was right without even being aware of it—from the rest. The righteous fed the hungry and thirsty, welcomed strangers, clothed the naked, cared for the sick, and visited those in prison. The righteous stand in a right relationship with Christ and with "the least of these," and their actions flow naturally from that relationship. Connected to the true vine that is Christ, they bear much fruit, a harvest of righteousness.

. . . for the glory and praise of God.

The purpose of all our discernment is not to make us pure for the sake of purity, or to get an "A" on some divine final exam. We begin with love—God's love for us, and our love for God and for one another. Our response to that love—our worship and praise, our discernment, and our faithful lives—is for the glory and the praise of God. By aligning ourselves with God, being in tune with God, we worship God truly. We praise God through our words and our deeds.

Pause for reflection

☙ *What elements of discernment does Paul emphasize in this prayer?*

☙ *Could you pray this prayer for your congregation today? If yes, take a few minutes right now to pray it, lifting your congregation and its discernment to God.*

LEARNING FROM THE EARLY CHURCH

In the stories from Acts we see the early church engaging in discernment for a variety of purposes: choosing leadership, hearing a call to mission work, finding a way through a controversial issue. Details are limited and differ in each situation, but we begin to see some threads. We see that the work of discernment went hand in hand with worship, and could involve such elements as prayer, fasting, silence, sharing faith stories, and weighing experience and Scripture.

In the passage from 1 Corinthians, we hear Paul encouraging the church to test and discern. He does not go into much detail about how to do it. We notice that it is something the congregation is to do together, and that there does not seem to be a distinction between worship and discernment. They are not two separate activities, but are interwoven. Together the worshippers are to proceed in a peaceable and orderly fashion, with attentive listening to God and to each other. It is not a matter of finding the lowest common denominator that everyone can tolerate, or of arguing with each other until everyone has been persuaded that one point of view is correct. Instead, all are to learn, to be encouraged, and to be built up.

Like the early Christians in Philippi, we modern Christians have not yet become all that we might be. We have yet to grow into the fullness of Christ, and our communities struggle with quarreling, dissensions, and factions, just as the early church did. Paul's prayer for the Philippians is one that can also be prayed for us. Its vision underscores the communal nature of discernment and makes the link between the gifts of the Spirit—including that of overflowing love—and our discernment. It keeps our focus on God and all that can be hoped for as our love overflows more and more.

We have looked at these three biblical voices in order to better understand the spiritual discipline of discernment. These congregations are discerning many different types of things: leadership issues, ministry directions, prophecies, lifestyle issues, "hot topics," and more. They do not follow any one, tidy technique; there is no "one right way" that guarantees genuine discernment. There is greater concern expressed that discernment happen than there are specifics given about how discernment is done. Still, as we consider these passages and the message they might carry for congregations of today, we can lift out several essentials.

Congregational discernment is intertwined with worship. Discernment and worship are two sides of the same coin. This means more than including a ten-minute sermon discussion time on Sunday morning, or bookend prayers to open and close our business meetings. Prayer, fasting, song, sharing faith stories, attentive silence, and other similar activities are all integral to the movement of discernment, making possible the moments of discernment.

Congregational discernment is a communal activity. In many cultures this would be so obvious that there would be no point in attaching the qualifiers "communal" or "congregational" to discernment. In our highly individualistic North American context, it is not idly redundant to emphasize it one more time. Our discernment grows from our relationship with God and our relationships with each other. It is this community that receives the gifts of the Spirit that make discernment possible. To nurture a climate of discernment, we must nurture these relationships.

Congregational discernment is an ongoing activity. As individuals and as faith communities, we are works-in-progress. Not only are we changing, but the world around us is also changing, and the Spirit is active in the world. In our discernment we discover where our ever-creative God is already at work in the world and where we are invited to join in.

Congregational discernment is done for the glory and praise of God. It is done *with* praise, in a spirit of worship, and it is done *for* praise. We are responding to the love and grace we receive from God, wanting to align ourselves with God's work in the world. We listen for God's song so that our decisions and our actions might be in tune with God. We discern so that our words and our deeds will give glory and praise to God.

DIALOGUE: TWO FOOLS FOR CHRIST

God

Additional readers: Computer Expert

Props: fancy calculator, colorful tie

T: Hi! I'm Theophilus.

A: And I'm Amadeus.

T: We're pilgrims on a journey.

A: Two fools for Christ who wander the world,

T: trying to put into words what can't be put into words,

A: trying to understand mystery and paradox and talk about them with people like you.

T: So, Amadeus, what's the word for today?

A: The word for today, Theophilus, is . . . *God*!

T: God? You mean God like in master of the universe, creator of heaven and earth, ruler of the stars and angels?

A: Yep, God.

T: Father, Son, and Holy Ghost?

A: That's the one.

T: You don't believe in small talk, do you?

A: Hey, it's not my idea. It's theirs *(Indicates group)*.

T: Theirs?

A: Remember? This is the group that is talking about dis-*cern*-ment *(With arm swing)*.

T: So what's that got to do with God?

A: Everything! At least when you're talking about congregational discernment. Don't you remember? It's all about being in tune with God and listening for God's song.

T: Oh, right, this is starting to come back now. It's aligning your decisions and actions with God, right?

A: Now you're cooking.

T: Okay, just hang on a minute. *(Pulls out fancy calculator and starts punching numbers)*.

A: Umm, Theophilus?

T: *(Still punching industriously)* Yes?

A: *What* are you doing?

T: I'm just trying to set up a little program.

A: A program?

T: Yeah, on my calculator here.

A: I can see it's a calculator. But what do you mean, a program? What has that got to do with God and discernment?

T: See, I just had this great idea. Discernment is all about getting our actions and decisions in line with who God is and what God is doing in the world, right?

A: (*Bewildered*) Yeah . . .

T: So, if I can just get God pinned down in a nifty little formula here, then any time we have a decision we need to discern, we can run this program and see how it compares!

A: Hey, great idea! Let me see (*Peers over T's shoulder*).

T: Okay, here's what I've got: God = love + justice + . . . what else?

A: If it's a formula it probably needs an N or a Z or a cosine or something.

T: (*Punching*) It doesn't seem to want to . . .

A: You know, I think we need some help.

T: Yeah, is there a computer expert in the house? (*Computer Expert comes up.*)

A: Could you give us a hand with this?

T: We just want to get God down as a neat little formula so we can match our decisions with the formula.

A: It sure would make discernment a lot easier.

T: Yeah, you'd be doing a great service to all humankind.

CE: (*Shrugging helplessly*) I wish I could help, but I just can't.

T: Why not?

A: Yeah, why not? You're a good programmer.

CE: Well, thanks. The real problem is that you can't fit God into a tidy little formula. God is too big and too real to fit into a program. You can't capture God with numbers any more than we could turn *you* into a tidy formula.

A: I guess it would be kind of hard to condense "master of the universe, creator of earth and sea," and all that.

T: So no go with the program, huh?

CE: I'm afraid not. (*T tosses calculator back into the kit sack*)

T: So how *do* we go about this discernment business?

A: Yeah, how do we know what is in tune with God?

CE: Well, I'm no expert, but maybe you could think about it more like a relationship than a program.

A: What do you mean?

CE: Well, like . . . like . . . (*Inspired*) like trying to figure out the right gift to give someone.

T: The right gift?

CE: Yeah. Like my friend, Judy. She pays attention to things I say and she knows what I like to do and what I really hate. And she's really creative. She comes up with gifts for me that I never would have thought of getting for myself, but somehow they are just what I want. They are a perfect fit for me.

A: Oh, I know what you mean! Like this tie—isn't it just *me*? Theophilus found it for my birthday.

T: Or this hat! Amadeus found it in a used clothing store and knew right away it was just what I needed.

CE: That's the idea! You can't put that kind of knowledge in a formula or figure it out with your calculator. You know each other and so you know what to give each other.

A: And that's what discernment is like?

CE: Well, analogies are never perfect, but yeah, discernment is like figuring out the right gift for God.

T: But how are we supposed to figure out the right kind of gift for God?

CE: Well, why not the same way my friend figures out gifts for me? Listen to what God says and pay attention to what God likes and what God really hates.

A: But how are we supposed to do that when God isn't right here?

T: Yeah, it's not like we can take God out to the store and pay attention to what God oohs and aahs over.

CE: I *did* say analogies are never perfect. You have to listen for God in other ways—prayer, reading the Bible, attentive silence, observing nature, talking with others who are listening for God.

T: And what if we get it wrong?

CE: It happens. That's why we need to keep listening. Fortunately God is in the forgiveness business. Don't look so discouraged! Think what joy there is in finding the right gift for someone you love (*Returns to seat*).

A: You know, Theophilus, the Computer Expert is right. It *is* fun finding the right gift.

T: Yeah, when I found that tie for you, I did a jig right on the spot.

A: So did I when I found that hat for you! The check-out lady thought I was pretty strange.

T: I can't imagine why. Amadeus, do you really think discernment is like finding the right gift for God?

A: Sounds like a good way to think about it.

T: Okay, then, let's go and see what we can figure out. See you folks later.

A: After a while, crocodile.

(*They go out, ad-libbing and making a list, similar to: "Okay, God's into peace and justice and all that stuff. Really dislikes lies. No burnt offerings, remember?"*)

CHAPTER 3

Worship God Truly

TAKE DELIGHT

For many months the small church fellowship group I was part of had been practicing a modified *lectio divina*. *Lectio divina* is an ancient church practice, a way of reading Scripture thoughtfully and prayerfully, allowing time and space for encountering the living God through the written word. Those doing *lectio divina* begin by entering a time of prayer, opening themselves to God, then slowly reading a passage of Scripture out loud until a word or phrase stands out for them, speaking to them in a special way. Then they stop and meditate on that word or phrase, savoring it, and letting it resound in their hearts. Then comes a response to God in prayer, closing with resting silently in God's presence.

Normally this is all done alone, but my small group had been using a group version of *lectio divina* as a way of spending time with Scripture together. The details of the method had taken some getting used to, but by this point we were comfortable with the process. I laid claim to the four-month-old baby of one of our participants and prepared for the *lectio*, holding Sydney in my lap. Sydney was just at the stage where she loved to interact with people, gazing into my face with her bright brown eyes. I wrinkled my nose at her and she gave me her wide toothless grin as Lois began leading us through the passage, inviting us to open ourselves in prayer.

The usual recommendation for group *lectio divina* is to choose a short passage, just a couple of verses. But Lois had chosen a longer passage that evening, Deuteronomy 30:9b–14:

> For the Lord will again take delight in prospering you, just as he delighted in prospering your ancestors, when you obey the Lord your

God by observing his commandments and decrees that are written in this book of the law, because you turn to the Lord your God with all your heart and with all your soul. Surely, this commandment that I am commanding you today is not too hard for you, nor is it too far away. It is not in heaven, that you should say, "Who will go up to heaven for us, and get it for us so that we may hear it and observe it?" Neither is it beyond the sea, that you should say, "Who will cross to the other side of the sea for us, and get it for us so that we may hear it and observe it?" No, the word is very near to you; it is in your mouth and in your heart for you to observe.

As usual, she read it through aloud once, so that we could hear the whole passage. Then she handed the Bible with the marked passage to the person next to her, and invited us all to listen for a word or phrase that stood out for us as we heard it read a second time.

I listened to the reading while smiling down at Sydney, who joyfully smiled back. "Take delight" leapt out, echoing in my ear. I savored it during the moments of silence, delighting in my interchange with Sydney as she gave an even broader grin and a joyful silent chuckle, her eyes wide.

We went around the circle, briefly saying the words that had struck us: "heart and soul" . . . "the word is very near" . . . "turn" . . . "take delight." Lois passed the Bible to still another reader, and invited us to hear the passage yet again, this time listening for how the passage touched our lives. I closed my eyes and listened to the third reading. When I opened them during the silence that followed, there was Sydney, still gazing up, still full of joy at the chance to exchange a silent laugh.

It struck me that the word *was* very near. In Sydney's face, I saw the face of God. And it shaped how I heard the passage. At its core is relationship. The Lord takes delight when we turn to God with all our heart and soul, seeking God's face. Our actions and obedience can then be shaped by this interaction. God is able to write the new covenant on our hearts. We are not painstakingly obeying rules and regulations because we are afraid of what will happen if we do not behave, or because we hope to earn God's love. Our obedience flows from who we know God to be and from who we are becoming, as children of God. God yearns for this interchange of delight.

Relationship with God is at the core of congregational discernment. Faithful discipleship does not come from finding the right formula, but from seeking the face of God and taking delight together. It is fruit and words and deeds that grow authentically from that relationship. Of course, the relationship is not always as clear as looking into the laughing face of an infant. Our response to God is not always unalloyed delight; we do not yet see face to face. Sometimes God feels distant, remote, or unreal. God is both intimately known and awesomely unknown. But as individuals and as congregations, we can find ways to deepen our relationship with God, to better recognize God's song and to distinguish it from the static around us.

THE MYSTERY OF GOD

Images of God. George Burns wryly chomping a cigar in the movie, "O God." The majestic painted hand reaching out to Adam's hand on the Sistine Chapel ceiling. The bearded old man seated on a throne in the sky. The still, small voice. The Eastern Orthodox icon of three elongated figures standing together. The lion Aslan in the Narnia stories. The loving Mammy in her rocking chair. The ever-flowing water of life, pouring out in a life-giving stream. The arms-spread-wide Christ who knows everyone's stories.

Tucked away in my memory, like the catch-all cupboard in my hallway, is an odd collection of many little bits and pieces, a mish-mash of images of God. They come from many different places—the culture around me, things I have read or seen, the ways others have tried to explain their experience of God, and my own times of encounter with God. Some images I resonate with, others I reject, but still they are all there, higgledy-piggledy in my mental cupboard, and they all have some effect on my understanding of God. Each of us—even the most systematic of theologians—carries such a mental cupboard, sharing some images with others in our culture and having others that are unique to our own experience.

Not all the bits and pieces we carry are equal. Some deeply shape our life and faith, while others are peripheral. Some bring healing and new life, while others are actively negative, blocking our relationship with God. Some are consistent and true to the living God who is beyond all images, while others lead us astray into sterile wastes. True encounters with God, insights, and holy images are all mixed up with false, inadequate, and unworthy images. One task—and privilege—of our spiritual formation as individuals is the ongoing effort to spring-clean our cupboards.

The same is true of congregations. The images we carry influence our discernment. One task—and privilege—of our spiritual formation as congregations is the recurring effort of throwing our cupboards open to the fresh, spring breeze of the Spirit. We want to be in tune with the living God, not with a false image. At the same time, we cannot fall into the trap of thinking we have God all figured out. We can never fully explain, or describe, or understand God. In order to do so, we would have to be God. The living God is mystery, always unknown. We cannot carry God around tucked cozily in our pocket, like a lucky rabbit's foot, or a predictable formula. God is always much more than we can fathom, more than any image we carry.

So how can we be in tune with this unknowable God? How can we take delight together? We can, because while God is mystery and unknown, God is also known. It may be easier to talk about this paradox in something other than English. In Spanish, for example, there are two verbs that mean "to know." The verb *saber* means to have knowledge of, to know how to, or to know about something. The verb *conocer* is used for being acquainted with, or knowing, a person. We know God in the sense of *conocer*, not *saber*.

God is not a tidy set of propositions that we can learn off by heart, and know in the way we know a field of study. Nor is God a set of techniques, which we can master in the way we do mechanical skills. Knowing God is much more like knowing a person, with all the uncertainties, mystery, and surprises that that entails. The more fully we know someone, the more fully we are aware of how much more there is to know. And just as our knowledge of a person is shaded by who we are, the roles we are in, and the kind of interactions we have, our knowledge of God is also shaped in part by our own history, personality, and relationship with God. Though each of us encounters the living God, none of us can say we know all about God, or that our idea of God is a complete and perfect match with the living God.

God is mystery, unknown and yet known. Even though we do not know God the way we know the multiplication tables, we *do* know God.

The testimony of God's people over the ages is that God is a self-revealing God, seeking to know and to be known. Our writings and our stories, in Scripture and beyond, bear witness to the ways the people of God have experienced God repeatedly reaching out, calling us to new life and to more complete relationship, both as individuals and as a people. "I sought the Lord," we sing, "and afterwards I knew he moved my soul to seek him, seeking me." God is not content with remaining aloof in mystery, but reaches out, wanting to be known by us.

Pause for reflection

* *What are some of the images of God you carry?*

* *Which ones are life-giving? Which ones are sterile?*

* *Which images of God does your congregation use most frequently?*

THE SELF-REVEALING GOD

Over the centuries, Christians have talked about God in many ways. Influenced by the framework of Greek philosophical thought, we have focused at times on abstracts and universals, describing the nature of God by discussing divine attributes. The Greek philosophers' approach to understanding divinity was to work with definitions. By definition, the divine was understood as all-powerful, perfect, and unchanging, absolutely other than human. God is everything humans cannot be—omnipotent, omniscient, omnipresent, impassable.

In contrast, the Semitic approach to understanding God is much more implicit, embedded in holy writings, in ritual, story, and song. God is not defined by *otherness*, by being everything that humanity is not, but rather is understood in relationship to humans, as "being-with" the world. God reaches out to people, saying, "You will be my people and I will be your God." God's transcendence and power are understood in temporal and ethical terms—God is the Eternal One, the Righteous

One. Power is not the basic defining aspect of God, but instead is used in the service of God's desire for mutual, interdependent relationship. God's will is based firmly in God's steadfast love and desire for right relationship.

God makes God-self known to us in the biblical story. It is not an explicit, systematic presentation, but a revelation to be discovered in stories, songs, prophecies, lament, and praise which are open to many interpretations and differing shades of meaning. We can see multiple interpretations already in the Old Testament, as priestly, wisdom, and prophetic views of God bring different emphases to their respective writings, and also in the New Testament, where four different gospels give us their different perspectives. Still, despite the many voices, there is a deep consistency. In their witness, we meet the One who reveals God-self as Creator, Christ, and Spirit, our triune God.

The word *triune* does not appear in the Bible, but it captures something of what we want to say about the God we meet in Scripture. In the first centuries of the Christian Church, believers struggled to put into words the way they experienced God as Father,[1] Son, and Holy Spirit, and they developed an understanding of God as the Trinity. Theologians have been trying to make it logical ever since. But we do not need to wrestle with theological complexities to recognize the cohesion found in the biblical story. We come to know the One God through the unity of Father, Son, and Holy Spirit. The character revealed in this three-fold unity has implications for our congregational discernment.

THE TRIUNE GOD

Love-spilling-over: God's Unchanging Will

The One whom Jesus called Father is revealed to us in the biblical story as the One who created the world and who continues to cradle it. In the words of Catharine LaCugna in her book, *God for Us*, "The God who *is* love does not remain locked up in the 'splendid isolation' of self-love but spills over into what is other than God, giving birth to creation and history."[2] This love-spilling-over God yearns for relationship, creating the world, calling out a people and making covenant with them, and repeatedly calling them back into relationship when they stray.

This is not a soft, anything-goes love. God cares passionately not only about the interaction between God-self and humans, but also for interactions between humans, and between humans and the rest of creation. Through psalmist and prophet and law-writer, we learn about God's concern for right relations, for justice and righteousness. It is an often repeated message: take care of the poor and the oppressed, be stewards of the earth, treat the stranger with hospitality, let justice roll down like waters and righteousness like an ever-flowing stream. When instead injustice and broken relationships prevail, God grows angry. But always, beyond the anger, God's steadfast love endures. Indeed, the anger is there *because* of God's steadfast love for us. This is the unchanging melody of the song God sings us, a melody of justice for the poor and oppressed, peace and well-being for all creation, right relationship with God and with each other. God's steadfast love and care for creation is the unchanging face of God's will.

This melody of justice and righteousness has implications for our congregational discernment. The ground in which our discernment takes place is one of relationship with God and with each other. Long before any particular decision, we can nurture those relationships. As a congregation, we regularly come together in worship, where we may encounter God through song, prayer, confession, and hearing the Word, through communion and other rituals, through movement, art, and music. As a congregation, we can also nurture the spiritual formation of individuals in many ways: through spiritual directors, mentors, Sunday school classes, small groups, service projects, and more. Many of these also serve to strengthen the bonds between us, as do more social interactions.

We can also nurture relationships, divine and human, in the midst of discernment. Discussion of a particular decision may be interwoven with attentive silence, drawing the meeting back to a focus on God, and creating space for the working of the Spirit. Mennonites, along with many other denominations, have been introduced to Worshipful-Work, an approach developed by Charles Olsen and his associates that interweaves worship with decision making. As congregations we can seek out approaches that help us keep a broader perspective than any particular decision, remembering God's unchanging melody and the underlying purpose of our discernment.

We can also be attentive to our horizontal relationships with each other as we discern together, avoiding approaches that pit side against side. As Paul wrote to the quarreling Galatians,

> For you were called to freedom, brothers and sisters; only do not use your freedom as an opportunity for self-indulgence, but through love become slaves to one another. For the whole law is summed up in a single commandment, "You shall love your neighbor as your-self." If, however, you bite and devour one another, take care that you are not consumed by one another (Galatians 5:13–15).

Pause for reflection

❧ How do you nurture your own relationship with God? With others?

❧ How does your congregation nurture relationships among its members? With God?

❧ What relationship-building elements does your congregation include in its current discernment and decision making?

Power with Vulnerability: God's Interactive Will

The One God is also revealed to us in the life, death, and resurrection of Jesus. In the biblical stories about Jesus, we encounter one who walked and talked with the "little ones" of the land, who shared table fellowship with sinners and tax collectors, who healed and challenged and called everyone into the kingdom of heaven. We encounter one who made himself vulnerable, risking suffering and humiliation in faithful obedience to his Father. And we encounter one who died forsaken and rejected, executed like a common criminal on a wooden cross.

"We proclaim Christ crucified, a stumbling block to Jews and foolishness to the Gentiles," Paul wrote to the church in Corinth (1 Corinthians 1:23). Death on the cross would seem to cancel any claim for Jesus being the Messiah. Yet God raised him up, putting a divine stamp of approval on Jesus' life, teachings, and death. He is the king who rode in to Jerusalem on a humble donkey, not a war-stallion; the one who refused to use the sword or to call in angel-battalions to save his life; the one who taught us to love our enemies and to do good to those who would harm us. He met the attack of this world's powers and principalities with vulnerability, accepting even death on the cross.

And then, as Peter tells the crowd at Pentecost, "God raised him up, having freed him from death, because it was impossible for him to be held in its power. . . . Therefore let the entire house of Israel know with certainty that God has made him both Lord and Messiah, this Jesus whom you crucified" (Acts 2:24, 36). The crucified Christ turns our assumptions about power upside down. Power as the world understands it is based in fear. It dominates and controls, and has violence as a close companion. But divine power is defined first and foremost by love. God is *not* enslaved by fear, and thus can risk compassion and vulnerability. This is power that death cannot quench, power that bursts the bonds of death. It is power that is not self-contained absoluteness, but instead is relational, giving and receiving, willing to be affected by the other. This power does not suffer through passive acceptance, but resists evil with everything it can—everything *except* evil's own weapons of dominating, coercive power.

Having had our understandings of divine power turned upside-down by Jesus' life, death, and resurrection, we become aware of power in the midst of our discernment. Power is a complex issue and takes many shapes. Power can be generative, helping us to accomplish good things. It can also be domineering and deadening. As congregations, we can nurture an internal awareness of how we use power, avoiding actions that are manipulative, coercive, or controlling. We can find ways to call out and affirm the appropriate use of power, building one another up in love.

The face of power that we see in Jesus' life, death, and resurrection is the same power expressed in creation and covenant. God did not create us as marionettes, willy-nilly doing God's will. God set aside absolute power in order to maintain the integrity of relationship. God created us with free will. God's deep desire is that we freely acknowledge our relationship as children of God, committing ourselves to walk in Jesus' Way, and aligning ourselves with God's vision for the world.

But there is choice, and some choose to turn from God and some work with alternate visions. Sometimes, despite the best intentions, we wander from the Way. There *is* evil in the world. God constantly needs to be creative, working with God's children to bring light into darkness, and healing into brokenness, constantly mending, revising, and improvising. This is the interactive face of God's will. God's unchanging vision of justice and right relationship is worked out in relationship with creation. Jesus Christ is the Lamb whose death has already redeemed us and conquered the power of evil, but we also live in the "not yet" time. The reconciliation of all creation is not yet complete. God continues improvising the way the unchanging melody is sung in a particular setting, and invites us to add our complex harmonies to the divine song.

Given the presence of evil in the world, our participation in the song has implications for congregational discernment. We are co-workers with God in responding to evil. We are responsible for calling out to God when we encounter injustice and brokenness. The book of Psalms shows us one way to do this. More than half the psalms are laments—songs where the psalmist calls out to God, naming specific complaints and making specific requests, all the while trusting that God will act for justice and right relationship, in a manner worthy of praise. We too need to name before God the wrongs that we see, calling on God to right what is wrong. We also need to name our own sins and failings, trying to stand honestly before God, trusting in God's grace to "turn us round right." Whether done in gathered worship or in other settings, lifting our laments and confessions to God can be an important step in congregational discernment.

God constantly improvises to mend the damage done by injustice and unrighteousness. We are called to join in that work, seeking our role in the mending. We are ambassadors for Christ, sharing in the work of healing and reconciliation. We too will need to improvise as the context changes around us, discerning what will most authentically embody the unchanging song in this time and place. We need to be attentive to where God is already at work in the world and align ourselves with that. This is why congregational discernment is an ongoing activity. We never get it figured out once and for all because we, and the world around us, are always changing, and God chooses to interact with us and with the world.

Pause for reflection

🌢 *Where have you experienced generative, life-giving power in your congregation? Where have you encountered the dominating, coercive use of power?*

🌢 *Where do you encounter injustice and brokenness? What laments and confessions would you like to lift to God?*

Empowering Presence: God's Invitational Will

Through the biblical story, and through our own experiences, we glimpse the role of the Holy Spirit. Through the Spirit, the love-spilling-over, risk-taking God reaches out, drawing together a people, transforming and renewing them, and reconciling them with God and with each other. God is personally present in our lives, and active in our midst, through the agency of the Spirit. The Spirit is the one who knows the thought of God, teaching, challenging, and guiding us into truth. It is the Spirit who helps transform us, guiding our spring-cleaning. It is through the Spirit that we receive gifts for building up the Body in love; it is the Spirit that knits the diverse many into one Body. It is through the Spirit that we receive fruits of love, joy, peace, patience, kindness, goodness, faithfulness, gentleness, and self-control. It is through the Spirit that we sing God's song.

Through the Spirit, at times we receive specific calls. God reaches out, inviting us to take up a particular piece of God's vision for the world. It may be an invitation to a one-time activity ("Get up and go to the street called Straight"—the directions Ananias receives in Acts 9:11), or a call that shapes one's entire life (the invitation to be filled with the Holy Spirit which Ananias brings to Paul). Congregations as well as individuals receive invitations, which again may be to a one-time activity or to changes that shape the congregation's life and identity. In Acts 11:27–30, the church in Antioch hears the invitation to send aid to the believers living in Judea. In Acts 10–11 and 15, we learn of the lengthy effort of the church in Jerusalem to understand what the Spirit was saying to them about how to receive Gentiles into the church.

Such invitations did not only happen long ago and far away. The Spirit is still active in our midst, inviting us to fulfill specific tasks and to grow in new ways, and then gifting and empowering us for carrying these out. This is the invitational face of God's will. God calls us to add our Spirit-led improvisations to the divine song and, with the Spirit, to carry this song to places of cacophony and discord.

This work of the Spirit also has implications for our congregational discernment. Congregations need to make space for the Spirit—space for the Spirit to transform and renew us, space for the Spirit to tap us on the shoulder and invite us to move in sometimes unexpected directions. This may mean something as simple—and as complicated—as learning to listen to others with the expectation that the Holy Spirit may be speaking through what they have to say, rather than half-listening and instead working on our own speech. It may mean a shift in orientation, from seeing our decision making as primarily about the bottom line to seeing it as an opportunity to listen for the leading of the Spirit. It may involve setting aside time for individuals or small groups to study and pray in preparation for a particular discussion. It may include incorporating prophetic listening through Quaker-style silence, the repetitive singing of a meditative song, or guided work with a passage of Scripture. The methods used will vary, but our goal is to find ways that help us to work together with a spirit of openness, holding ourselves ready to pay attention to and to respond to the Spirit's leading.

Pause for reflection

❧ When and how have you experienced the Holy Spirit in your own life?

❧ How does your congregation open itself to the Spirit's guidance?

SEEKING GOD'S FACE

Congregational discernment is based in our relationship with the living God. The children of God seek God's face, taking delight in aligning their choices and actions with God's vision for the world. The recurring spring-cleaning of our images and understandings of God helps us to grow in this relationship, repeatedly transformed by the Spirit, as we grow into the fullness of Christ. "Speaking the truth in love, we must grow up in every way into him who is the head, into Christ, from whom the whole body, joined and knit together by every ligament with which it is equipped, as each part is working properly, promotes the body's growth in building itself up in love" (Ephesians 4:15–16).

With congregational discernment, we are listening for God, wanting our decisions to be in tune with God. We want both the moment of discernment and the movement that leads to decision to be shaped by God's song. Our images and understandings of God influence this discernment. Deepening our awareness of the triune God will strengthen our concern for justice and right relationships, not only as we look at the outcome of a particular decision, but also in the ways we interact together. It will affect how we use power, and influence the ways we speak truth to one another. It will encourage us to make space for the Spirit to transform us, softening our hard hearts and opening our eyes to our own areas of blindness, space for active listening for the Spirit, guiding us in our discernment.

NOTE

[1] Jesus is the one who dared to address the Holy One as Father. This masculine language is problematic today, especially for those abused by their own fathers or by the patriarchal system. Yet in avoiding it, we lose an important emphasis on relationship. While for the most part I prefer gender-neutral language for God, this is one setting where the use of Father seems warranted. Perhaps we can hear it in the sense of Matthew 23:9, "And call no one your father on earth, for you have one Father—the one in heaven."

[2] Catharine Mowry LaCugna, *God for Us: The Trinity and Christian Life* (San Francisco, California: HarperCollins Publishers, 1991), 353.

God's Will

Additional readers: Doctor, Martha (wise older woman)

Props: For this dialogue, both Amadeus and Theophilus enter wearing backpacks in addition to the kit sack they carry. Theophilus's contains a big stick, a wind-up clock, and five or six old tapes. Amadeus's contains the *Diagnostic and Statistical Manual for Mental Disorders IV* (or you can improvise with a large, heavy reference or textbook), a blueprint and five or six old tapes

T: Hi! I'm Theophilus.

A: And I'm Amadeus.

T: We're pilgrims on a journey.

A: Two fools for Christ who wander the world,

T: trying to put into words what can't be put into words,

A: trying to understand mystery and paradox and talk about them with people like you.

T: What's the word for today, Amadeus?

A: The word for today, Theophilus, is . . . *God's will.*

T: Whoof—God's Will! That's pretty heavy-duty stuff, isn't it? You know, I really get antsy when people start talking about God's Will. Usually it's just a sneaky way for them to get their own way.

A: Hmmm, maybe we'd better take a look at what you are carrying with you, Theophilus. Here, let me see what you've got in your backpack. (*Looks in T's backpack and pulls out big stick.*) Look at this!

T: Yes! That's it. People wave "God's Will" around like a big stick.

A. Well, that's certainly one image many people carry with them. Here, let me help you take off this backpack. I think we'd better see what other images you're carrying around.

T: (*Starts rummaging, but interrupts to add*) You know, you'd better see what you are carrying, too, Amadeus (*A looks surprised, then discovers his/her backpack, removes it, and sets it on table and also starts rummaging*). What have *you* got?

A: Well, let's see. Oh—there's this (*Pulls out book*).

T: Wow! Now there's a tome. Let's see. *Diagnostic and Statistical Manual for Mental Disorders IV.* Mental disorders?

A: Well, you know. People hearing voices. I mean, they may *think* they are hearing God's voice, but they're really psychotic or hallucinating or something.

T: Hmmm . . . I guess that's true some of the time (*Pulls out wind-up clock*). Hey, look! How about this?

A: (*Taking and winding it*) Oh, yeah—I know that one. This is where we see God as the Divine Clockmaker, right?

T: Yeah—God created the world and the rules that run it and gave us reason to figure it all out and to figure out what we ought to do.

A: And then it's hands off, right? Just let the world run on its own.

T: That's it (*They watch the clock tick for a few seconds, then start rummaging again*).

A: Ha! Look—how about this one? (*Pulls out blueprint*)

T: That's the other extreme, isn't it? That's where we see God as totally in charge, with a precise idea of every least little thing that has to be.

A: And you had better figure it out right, or look out!

T: Time for the big stick, huh? Here, look—here's some old tapes.

A: How about that—I have some too. What are yours?

T: Let's see—well, this one is Aunt Eunice. She was always talking about God's will. And this one is labeled Mrs. Miller. Miller . . . Miller (*Searching memory*). Oh, I know—she was my sixth grade Sunday school teacher.

A: (*Looking over own tapes*) Here's *my* eighth grade Sunday school teacher, and this one is my friend Jim, and this is a sermon I heard once.

T: And here's the speech my parents always gave me, and here's my friend Carla. We sure carry around a lot of old tapes, Amadeus.

A: You can say that again, Theophilus.

T: We sure carry . . .

A: Oh, hush. Let's get them all out on the table here, along with all the other stuff (*Shakes out a few more tapes from the backpacks*).

T: Now what, Amadeus?

A: (*Scratching head*) You got me. They wanted us to talk about God's will, and we've been doing that.

T: Yeah, but where does it get us? This just looks like a junk heap.

A: Hmm . . . maybe we need to examine it in some way.

T: Examine it?

A: You know, give it a check up. See if it's healthy.

T: Healthy? Amadeus, it's just a bunch of symbols and old tapes and stuff.

A: Okay, so maybe we'd better see if *we're* healthy, carrying all this stuff around. Is there a doctor in the house?

Dr: (*Standing*) I'm a doctor, but I don't think I can help you.

A: (*Clutches chest*) You mean, it's fatal?!

Dr: No, no, you look perfectly healthy. But maybe you should con- sult a specialist.

T: (*Worried*) What kind of specialist?

Dr: Someone who can help you talk about God's will. Maybe some- one like Martha.

A: Who's Martha?

Dr: She's an older woman who is part of this congregation. She doesn't talk about God's will a whole lot, but she knows how to pray and how to listen. When we have decisions to make as a congregation, she usually has things to say that help us see the right way to go.

T: That sounds promising. Martha, could you come up here?

M: (*Comes up, flustered*) I wouldn't say I'm a *specialist*. I'm sure there are lots of people here who know more than I do.

A: That doesn't matter, if you can just give us some ideas on what to do with all this mess.

M: Looks to me like you need a good spring-cleaning. Maybe you should treat it like I do my medicine cabinet. It has medicines and supplies I really need, but there is also junk I've gathered along the way and bottles whose expiration dates are past and things that are just taking up space.

T: But how are we supposed to know which is which?

A: Yeah, there aren't any expiration dates on these things.

M: Now let me think. Maybe it's more like sorting my mail pile. There is always junk mail and bills that need to be paid and cata- logs I don't need. But then there are also letters from dear friends.

T: So what's the connection here?

M: Well, I can tell which are the letters from my friends because I know my friends well and recognize their handwriting and know what they sound like. Maybe you need to see which of these sym- bols and tapes and things match what we know about God.

A: Hmm, sort of like comparing new letters with old letters?

M: Yes—how does all this (*Gestures towards things on table*) fit with the old letters, with the messages we have from the prophets, and the apostles, and Jesus?

T: How does its' handwriting compare with Jesus' handwriting, so to speak?

M: Yes—and how does it fit with what we know of God in other ways? What kind of fruit does it produce?

A: Wait a minute—I thought we were talking about a mail pile, not an orchard.

M: It doesn't really matter. We're just trying to find some useful ways for thinking about it all.

T: So what kind of fruit do you mean?

M: The fruit of the Spirit, of course. Does it build up community? Does it help us grow in kindness and patience and gentleness and generosity? Does it bring about more justice and more well-being for everybody? Does it help us to love God and our neighbor?

T: Wow, all that?

A: Mostly all this stuff is just sitting here.

M: Now don't you fret. Spring-cleaning always feels like a real chore when you're getting started. But then it is all so clean and fresh afterwards that it gives you a real boost.

T: Well, I hope you're right.

A: Maybe we can leave all this stuff here for right now, and later maybe some of these folks can help us do some sorting of it all.

T: Yeah, I wonder what they are carrying in *their* backpacks?

M: Maybe we can all help each other with our spring-cleaning. It's more fun if you don't have to do it alone.

A: Sounds good to me.

T: Me, too. (*To group*) So bring your mops and buckets and discerning skills and we'll see you soon.

CHAPTER 4

Discerning God's Will

A LIVING SACRIFICE

The apostle Paul took delight in God's love and mercy. You can hear it in the background of the eleventh chapter of his letter to the Roman house churches. He writes of the wonder of the mercy that God has shown the Gentiles, and that he himself has experienced. He wrestles with the lack of response coming from his fellow Jews, but is convinced that they too will come to know God's mercy. He's so sure about God's wonder and mystery that it bursts out from him in a song of praise in Romans 11:33–36. Then he goes on:

> I appeal to you therefore, brothers and sisters, by the mercies of God, to present your bodies as a living sacrifice, holy and acceptable to God, which is your spiritual worship. Do not be conformed to this world, but be transformed by the renewing of your minds, so that you may discern what is the will of God—what is good and acceptable and perfect (Romans 12:1–2).

One response to God's mercies is to offer ourselves. Offering ourselves as a living sacrifice is our spiritual worship, or our reasonable service, as the King James Version has it. Whether we translate it as worship or service, the original Greek refers to the carrying out of religious duties. The true way to respond to God, the genuine way of serving and worshipping God, is by presenting our bodies as a living sacrifice.

This instantly brings up pictures of Christian martyrs about to be devoured by beasts in the Forum, but this is not primarily what Paul had in mind. We focus in on "sacrifice" and so hear it through the wrong filter. Our modern hearing is shaped by a setting in which ritual sacrifice is a vague historical oddity or something done in foreign lands. We are accustomed to using "sacrifice" in a metaphorical sense. We toss around phrases like, "It was a real sacrifice," or, "I sacrificed the best years of my life for you." When we use the word, we are not picturing something placed on the altar in offering to God. We are focusing on loss and on giving up something.

For Paul and his original listeners, ritual sacrifice was not a metaphor, but a vivid reality. In ritual sacrifice, some *object*—grain, a pigeon, a lamb—was dedicated and offered to God in atonement or thanksgiving or petition. Jews were familiar with the sacrifices that were offered at the Temple in Jerusalem. Gentiles were familiar with the ritual sacrifice that was a common element in the worship of Greco-Roman gods. In fact, the question of whether to eat meat that had been sacrificed to these gods was one cause of conflict in the early church. In 1 Corinthians, Paul addresses the question of whether or not it was acceptable to eat such meat; he touches on it again in Romans 14.

In calling for a living sacrifice, Paul is taking that very familiar concept of ritual sacrifice and standing it on its head. He keeps the idea of offering something to God, but what is offered has changed. True worship is not offering goats or pigeons or sheep to God. True worship is not doing all the right ritual duties. True worship is a *living* sacrifice, a joyful response to God in which we offer our whole selves. Instead of the ritual sacrifice of first century Judaism and Greco-Roman worship, we give glory and praise to God by our everyday living, all that we are, and say, and do. This idea is not new with Paul, of course. It is solidly based in his Jewish heritage where observant Jews recite the Shema morning and evening: "Hear, O Israel: the Lord is our God, the Lord alone. You shall love the Lord your God with all your heart, and with all your soul, and with all your might" (Deuteronomy 6:4–5).

Other New Testament writers also use the metaphor of sacrifice. The book of Hebrews is an extended sermon developing the idea that Jesus' death was the end of all ritual sacrifice. The author of Hebrews puts Psalm 40:6–7 in the mouth of Christ:

Consequently, when Christ came into the world, he said, "Sacrifices and offerings you have not desired, but a body you have prepared for me; in burnt offerings and sin offerings you have taken no pleasure. Then I said, 'See, God, I have come to do your will, O God' (in the scroll of the book it is written of me)" (Hebrews 10:5–7).

The passage goes on to explain that Jesus has abolished the first—the sacrifices—in order to establish the second—the doing of God's will. By Jesus' death, we have been cleansed, and the system of ritual sacrifice has been brought to an end. Christ leads us in the way; true worship is the doing of God's will. In chapters 12 and 13 we learn more about this "acceptable worship" (Hebrews 12:28). It includes pursuing peace and holiness, continuing in mutual love, being hospitable, remembering prisoners, being faithful in marriage, and living simply. It involves both our *words* and our *actions*:

Through [Jesus], then, let us continually offer up a sacrifice of praise to God, that is, the fruit of lips that confess his name. Do not neglect to do good and to share what you have, for such sacrifices are pleasing to God (Hebrews 13:15–16).

To worship God truly, we offer our whole selves as a living sacrifice, a sacrifice of praise that includes our words and our deeds. We give glory and praise to God by living everyday lives that are in tune with God's will.

BE DISCERNING

Faithful obedience to God's will, living in tune with God's desire for the world, puts us at odds with much of the way the present age does things. In the Romans passage, Paul goes on to alert his readers to the need for adopting a new perspective, a new way of seeing things. "Do not be conformed to this world, but be transformed by the renewing of your minds, that you may discern what is the will of God—what is good and acceptable and perfect" (Romans 12:2). The way of the world—the way of this present age—is not the same as the way of the Spirit. We have only to look around and see the mess the world is in to know that God's desire for peace, justice, and righteousness is not being lived out.

Have your eyes open, Paul says. Know that walking in God's way may mean taking a different path than others are following. Be discerning. Open yourselves to the work of the Spirit, who will be transforming you from the inside out, renewing your minds, changing your attitudes and your perspective and your way of seeing. As our minds are renewed and transformed by the Spirit, so too will our words and actions be transformed. The Anabaptists used the language of rebirth and the regenerated life to talk of this transformation. Through the Spirit, God's grace not only brings the believer to repentance and belief in the gospel, but also brings an inner regeneration that produces visible, outward good fruits.

This process of transformation of our inmost being and our outward actions is an ongoing one and is communal as well as individual. For individuals, it is a journey that begins before baptism and continues afterwards; for congregations it is a journey for the gathered body of those who already *are*, but also have *not yet* become a new people. It is a spiral: as we are transformed, we become better able to be aware of and in tune with the will of God, and to show it in our interactions with one another and with the world. We also become more fully aware of our need for continuing transformation in order to know and to do God's will. A living sacrifice and our ability to discern the will of God are tightly interconnected.

Being a living sacrifice can be costly praise. Sometimes this offering of our whole selves to God *does* lead to martyrdom. There were Christians who faced the beasts in the Forum, and there are Christians who still face death and persecution today. Jesus warned that those who truly wanted to be his followers would need to take up their cross daily. Paul and the writer to the Hebrews warn their readers not to be surprised when the way they are following leads them into suffering. There can be painful consequences to being part of a people whose new way of seeing puts them at odds with the present age. A living sacrifice calls for being a contrast-society, one that discerns between those words and deeds that are consistent with who God is and what God is doing in the world, and those that are not—a contrast-society that seeks to do God's will.

Pause for reflection

❧ *In what ways do you offer God a sacrifice of praise? Where does it happen through words? Where does it happen through deeds?*

❧ *Where do you see your congregation being a contrast-society?*

FRAMES OF UNDERSTANDING

With congregational discernment, we are seeking to know and to do God's will. This simple sentence, while true, can also become a major barrier to discernment. "God's will" is a term that carries a lot of weight. Some people can't hear it without flinching. Some find it deeply meaningful. For still others it is a complete mystery and hard to grasp. Just as we have a mental cupboard full of images of God, we have certain frameworks and ways of understanding "God's will." As with our images of God, our spiritual formation involves both the privilege and the responsibility of examining those images. In fact, the two are related. Our images of God and our assumptions about how God is at work in the world influence our understandings of God's will. While we each have our own unique combination of images and understandings of God's will, there are several broad frameworks that have developed over time. Our assumptions about how God interacts with the world are likely to be influenced by one or more of these frameworks. Sometimes we operate with several contradictory frameworks. Awareness of their strengths and weaknesses may help us to be more aware of our own filters and to better understand the perspective of others.

One framework has sometimes been called *determinism*. With this understanding, the dominant image is God as all-powerful sovereign, with the emphasis on power and control. All events are totally subordinate to God's guidance and control. God's will is described as a blueprint, or as the one correct way through a maze of rambling paths. The language of God's will comes easily to those influenced by this frame. The strength of this frame is its willingness to talk about God's involvement with the world, the trust that God is ultimately in control even in the midst of trouble and chaos, and its conviction that God is at work transforming the world. The drawback is that "God's will" can be used as a trump card, claiming superiority for one viewpoint, without any need for discernment. The language of "God's will" has been used to legitimize actions and perpetuate structures that have nothing to do with the reign of God, from the Crusades to slavery to sexual abuse to economic oppression.

Another framework is *deism*. With this frame, God is seen as clockmaker. God is understood to have created the universe and set it going with built-in rules, which enable it to develop and function without need for continuing divine presence or involvement. God's will is understood as these built-in rules, which can be discovered through the use of reason and observation. The strength of deism is its belief in an orderly world that can be explored through the exercise of our God-given gifts of reason and creativity. The drawback is that this framework makes it difficult to conceive of God as actively engaged with the world *now*. Those influenced by this frame may find it hard to see why prayer or spiritual formation should be an integral part of discernment.

Deism is a child of enlightenment rationalism, as is *modernism*, which sees no need to assume the existence of God or any reality beyond the concrete physical world. Since this worldview has no image of or place for God, it is not a framework in the same sense as the others. Nonetheless, it is a cultural stream that influences all North Americans to some extent. If we examine ourselves closely, we may discover that, whatever we *say* we believe about God's presence and activity in the world, our decisions and actions suggest that we are operating from a functional atheism, not really believing that God has anything to do with our discernment. One result of this worldview is that even in our churches some will find it difficult or incomprehensible to talk about God or about knowing and doing God's will.

More recently a new framework is developing, *postmodernism*. This worldview understands reality to integrate both the spiritual and material realms. It has not yet settled into an easily definable view of God and God's interaction with the world—God may be seen as a force, as the deep reality underlying all other reality, or simply as mystery and unknowable. Those influenced by this frame may talk about God (or at least about spirituality) more easily than those influenced by modernism, but they may also have a difficult time seeing God's will as something that can be known and done. The strengths of postmodernism are its respect for diversity, its critique of dominating power that bolsters one group at the expense of others, and its openness to mystery. The weaknesses of postmodernism include its tendency to slip into relativism, and the assumption that because no one person knows the whole truth, there *is* no whole truth. Discernment may seem pointless, rather than a communal activity to which we all contribute our own unique perspectives and insights.

Pause for reflection

❧ *What frameworks for understanding the world have influenced you?*

❧ *How have you experienced their strengths and weaknesses?*

❧ *How do you understand God to be at work in the world?*

BIBLICAL FRAMEWORK

In chapter three, we looked to the biblical writers for their multi-voiced witness to the One God, revealed to us in the unity of Father, Son, and Holy Spirit. We turn back to the same source for a deeper understanding of God's will.

In both Hebrew and Greek, there is no single phrase that is an exact equivalent for the English phrase, "God's will." In the Hebrew scriptures, specific references to God's will are rare. The Hebrew word *hefets* is occasionally translated as *will*, but more frequently appears as *delight*, or *pleasure*, or *desire*. We see it in verses like Jeremiah 9:24: "I act with steadfast love, justice, and righteousness in the earth, in these things I *delight*, says the Lord." *Ratson*, another word with meanings of *goodwill*, *favor*, *acceptance*, *desire*, and *pleasure*, is also sometimes translated as *will*. Both roots are at play in Psalm 40: "I *delight* (*hefets*) to do your *will* (*ratson*), O my God; your law is within my heart (v. 8). Or as the Jewish Publication Society translates the same verse: "To do *what pleases You*, my God, is my *desire*; Your teaching is in my inmost parts."

In the New Testament, *eudokia* echoes the Hebrew focus on what God delights in. Often translated as *gracious will* or God's *good pleasure*, it is closely related to the verb *eudokeo*, meaning *well pleased*, as in "You are my Son, the Beloved, with you I am *well pleased*" (Matthew 3:17, Mark 1:11, Luke 3:22).

The Greek term for *will* used most frequently in the New Testament is *thelēma*, or *thelēma theou*, will of God. *Thelēma* carries the meaning of desire or intention. While it can be used of either humans or God, most of the occurrences in the New Testament are in reference to God. This is the word Matthew uses in the Lord's Prayer: "Your *will* be done, on earth as it is in heaven" (Matthew 6:10).

Boulomai also means *desire* or *purpose*, with the added shading of reasoned planning. It is usually used about human wishes or plans, as in "Paul *wished* to go into the crowd, but the disciples would not let him" (Acts 19:30). It is also used about a dozen times to refer to God's plans or purpose, as in Acts 2:23: ". . . this man, handed over to you according to the definite *plan* and foreknowledge of God, you crucified and killed."

If we look at the many passages where these Hebrew and Greek words appear, we see a number of themes emerging:

For these writers, God's will does not narrowly refer to God's plans for the future. In our contemporary English usage, we often stress a future orientation over the eternal. When people ask, "What is God's will for me?" we assume they are looking ahead, wanting to make a decision about their next steps. We don't usually respond, "Love the Lord your God with all your heart and mind and soul, and love your neighbor as yourself." But this timeless emphasis on what delights God is an important element for our own understanding. God's will is not just God's intentions for the future, but the unchanging melody of all that gives God pleasure and delight.

Whether we talk of the eternal song or of intentions, God's deep desire is for reconciliation and relationship. This emphasis comes in a variety of wordings: God giving us birth (James 1:18), adopting us (Ephesians 1:5), not wanting any little ones lost (Matthew 18:14), not wanting any to perish but all to come to repentance (2 Peter 3:9). From Ephesians 1 we learn that this desire for right relationship is at the very heart of God's will: "With all wisdom and insight he has made known to us the mystery of his will, according to his good pleasure that he set forth in Christ, as a plan for the fullness of time, to gather up all things in him, things in heaven and things on earth" (v. 8b–10). We are called into relationship with God.

God's will is not something "out there" somewhere—it is a song that we too participate in here and now. Doing God's will is another strong theme, as in Matthew 7:21: "Not everyone who says to me, 'Lord, Lord,' will enter the kingdom of heaven, but only the one who does the will of my Father in heaven." Doing what delights God, joining in with God's deep desires for the world, brings us into new relationship with God and with each other. We are no longer strangers, but members of a new people, a new family: "Whoever does the will of God is my brother and sister and mother" (Mark 3:35). This is not through our own actions alone. As Paul wrote the Philippians, "It is God who is at work in you, enabling you both to will (*theleo*) and to work for his good pleasure (*eudokia*)" (2:13). The grace of God and the transforming work of the Spirit help us to desire and to do what God desires for the whole creation. The Spirit not only invites us into the song, but also teaches us how to sing.

The Bible does not give us a single image as a metaphor for God's will. Perhaps this is because in Greek and Hebrew "God's will" is not the proper noun that it has nearly become in English. When some people say it, you can almost see the capital letters forming: God's Will, practically an entity in itself. In contrast, the Bible has several words and phrases that are used for "God's will." We can help to keep this richness in mind by also using a variety of phrases for the same concept: God's deep desires, what God wants for the world, what delights God, and the heart and mind of God. We can also explore metaphors for "God's will," biblical and otherwise, which help capture this fuller understanding. We have been using the metaphor of God's song in this book. One possible biblical metaphor is the river of the water of life.

THE RIVER OF THE WATER OF LIFE

The Sunday school class was talking about God's will, and the discussion was lively. Several people spoke heatedly about ways the concept gets abused. Eric remembered his experiences as a development worker in Guatemala, trying to organize villagers into a cooperative. The way things were, the middlemen who transported goods into the city charged such high fees that the villagers were actually losing money nearly every time. "One old man refused to consider the idea of a cooperative," Eric said. "He insisted that it was God's will that he was poor."

Sharon was upset over a newspaper article about a local fire in which several children had died. The family's gas heat had been disconnected and the fire had started in a jury-rigged space heater. The mother had been out buying crack, and the grandmother was unable to get the children down from the second floor where they were sleeping. "I wasn't at the funeral," she said. "But the paper reported that the pastor told the mother that it was God's will those children had died and that she should look on it as her wake-up call."

Susan acknowledged that people often used the phrase "God's will" in ways that just didn't seem compatible with her own understanding of God, but she wasn't ready to abandon it because of that. She had fond memories of the years she and Eric had spent in Central America and the way a good friend always said "*Si Dios quiere*"—"If God is willing" whenever she talked of future plans. "Sure, some people just throw it in from habit," Susan said. "But for Marielena, it was a sincere recognition that God was bigger than her own ideas and arrangements. It was a way of saying that she was open to whatever God wanted to do through her."

Michael shrugged. He had been born with a congenital problem that severely affected his eyes, causing him difficulties much of his life. Recent surgery had worsened the situation. "I don't see any point in talking about God's will. I don't see God as being that hands-on and involved with what is happening in the world."

Some of the younger members in the class had been listening without saying much. One of them chimed in now, "I don't get what the big deal is. If it's a term that gets abused, let's throw it out. Why do we need to talk about God's will?"

"But we talk about God's will all the time," Mary argued. "What about the Lord's prayer? You know, 'Thy kingdom come, thy will be done on earth as it is in heaven'? If we are followers of Jesus, shouldn't we also be praying, 'Not my will, but yours, God'"?

Joan agreed, sharing something she had been talking about recently with her spiritual mentor. "I used to think of God's will as a tightrope I had to balance on very carefully. When I rejected that, I didn't want to use the phrase at all. But my mentor thinks it is important to be able to talk freely about God's will. She had me listen to a taped sermon by Gordon Cosby from Church of the Saviour in Washington, D.C., and the image he uses is becoming deeply meaningful to me." She went on to share with the class this way of thinking of God's will as the river of the water of life.

In the vision of the new Jerusalem in Revelation, the angel shows John a river, bright as crystal, which flows from the throne of God and of the Lamb. Echoing a similar vision in Ezekiel 47, this river is the water of life. In Ezekiel, it starts as a small stream, barely up to the prophet's ankles, but it grows and deepens—knee deep, then waist deep, and then a river too deep to cross. It flows all the way to the sea, and where it enters the stagnant waters of the sea become fresh and sweet. Living things gather on its shore and fish fill the waters; along its banks are all kinds of trees for food. The tree of life is among them; its leaves are for the healing of the nations.

"My mentor tells me to think of this river when I think of God's will," Joan told them. "It is the deep longing of God's heart for the world and all it can be, a place where stagnant waters become fresh and sweet, where living things gather and find abundance, where there is healing and new life. Instead of balancing on my tightrope, I try to become aware of the river and let myself flow with the river."

Pause for reflection

৯ *What images of "God's will" do you carry?*

৯ *What images of God's will are most prevalent in your congregation?*

❧ Do any of these images need spring-cleaning?

~

KNOWING GOD'S WILL

With congregational discernment, we are seeking to know and to do God's will. But how do we recognize God's will? How do we know what delights God? We turn to God's self-revelation in the written Word—the Bible—and the living Word—Jesus Christ. By immersing ourselves in the Word we learn the unchanging message of God's love for creation. We take God's teaching into our hearts, allowing ourselves to be shaped by God's vision of a world filled with justice, peace, and right relationships. Jesus, the one with whom God was well pleased, is our key to that vision. He reveals what delights God in his teachings, in the example of his faithful life and death, and through the good news of his resurrection. In Jesus we see the face of God.

For the Jews, God's desires were learned through the Torah—the teachings, or law, of the first five books of the Bible. What pleases or displeases God could also be heard in the words of the prophets and seen in the interactions of God and Israel through the histories and other writings. Jesus shared this foundation. In Luke's Gospel, Jesus announces his mission by reading from the prophet Isaiah. In Matthew, he tells his followers, "Do not think that I have come to abolish the law or the prophets; I have come not to abolish but to fulfill" (Matthew 5:17). In arguments with the scribes and Pharisees, he repeatedly shows his deep familiarity with the teachings of the Scriptures. Jesus continually pushes his listeners, including us, to reach for the deep meaning in Scripture. What is it that truly delights God? What does God desire from us? Whether arguing about Sabbath, or divorce, or hand washing, Jesus urges his listeners to focus on "the weightier matters of the law: justice and mercy and faith" (Matthew 23:23).

Jesus regularly spent time apart in silence and prayer. His disciples recognized the importance of this for his ministry and they asked him to teach them about prayer. Jesus also taught his followers to be alert to the signs of the times, to recognize what God was doing in the world around them. He promised them the Spirit of truth, who would guide them into all they needed to know. Our congregational discernment should also include space for prayer, for paying attention to what God is doing in the world, and for holding ourselves open to the Holy Spirit.

The Spirit aids us in developing our own relationship with God, both as individuals and as congregations. We open ourselves to transformation by the Spirit through prayer, silence, song, and more. We learn God's vision for the world through Scripture and through the Spirit at work in the gathered body of believers. The Spirit writes God's teachings on our hearts, helps us to weigh the words of the prophets among us, and gives us the gifts we need to join God's work.

We also learn God's will by stepping out in faith. Knowing God's will is only half the challenge. We can't really know or understood it until we attempt to live it. We come to a clearer understanding of God's will through risking response—trying, sometimes failing and needing to make corrections, and sometimes living in faithful congruence with God's desires for the world. We learn God's will by listening for God's song and by joining in, singing praise to God through our words and through our deeds.

The People of God

Additional readers: Two children (If two children are not available, parts could be done by two people wearing large labels proclaiming them as Child 1 and Child 2.)

Props: Pad of paper and fancy pen

T: Hi! I'm Theophilus.

A: And I'm Amadeus.

T: We're pilgrims on a journey.

A: Two fools for Christ who wander the world,

T: trying to put into words what can't be put into words,

A: trying to understand mystery and paradox and talk about them with people like you.

T: So, Amadeus, what's the word for today?

A: The word for today, Theophilus, is . . . *party*!

T: Party? Are you sure? I thought today's word was *The people of God*.

A: Well, it was. But what is there to say about the people of God? I mean, the people of God are those who respond to God's invitation to come be part of God's family, right? And when they all come together, at the end of time, it will be a big party, right?

T: I thought it was going to be a day of judgment.

A: Well, that too. But then afterwards there will be a big celebration. A big family reunion. A wedding banquet.

T: Hey, sounds like fun.

A: That's what I think. So I thought maybe we should start getting ready.

T: Getting ready? How?

A: I thought maybe God could use a helping hand.

T: What do you mean?

A: Well, there are an awful lot of people in the world.

T: That's for sure.

A: So I thought we could get started on the invitation list. You know, make some suggestions, jot down a few names. Maybe make some suggestions about seating arrangements at the banquet. After all, God has a lot to keep track of.

T: And who better to give a helping hand than two upright fools like us?

A: Exactly. (*Pulls out pad and pen*) So, who do we want at our table?

T: Well, put down our names, of course.

A: Of course (*Writes with a flourish*).

T: And let's see . . . how about Mother Teresa?

A: Oh, good one.

T: And then there's the pastor here, [name].

A: And my sister Trudy.

T: Oh, and my good friend, Jim.

(*They continue suggesting a series of names, with A scribbling them down: And John. Ashley. Pete. Valerie . . .*)

T: What about that family down the street, the ones from overseas?

A: Oh, I don't think so, do you? They don't even speak the same language we do. I'm sure they would be much more comfortable somewhere else.

T: Well, what about Tom?

A: Oh, Theo, you mean you didn't hear about Tom? I don't like to say it out loud, but everyone says that he . . . (*Whispers in T's ear, who looks startled*).

T: Well, no, I guess he isn't likely to be on the invitation list, is he? I certainly wouldn't put him there anyway.

A: How about Joyce?

T: Oh, please. Not at our table. She's so opinionated. And she's not really theologically sound, is she?

A: And for sure we don't want to put Bob down. He's just too . . .
(A is interrupted by two children tugging on his shirt.)

C1: Excuse me, mister.

A: What's that? What do you want?

C1: I heard you say you were making a list for God's party.

A: That's right. We're busy, important people. Gotta give God all the help we can, you know.

T: That's right. Help plan the seating, that sort of thing.

C2: That's what we don't understand. My Mommy says the host is the one who plans the party and invites the guests.

A: Well, er, . . . that's true.

T: But we're not planning the party. We're just sort of helping out.

C1: But how can you figure out the seating arrangements for God's party? Last week our Sunday school teacher taught us that parable about a banquet . . .

C2: You know, the one where people come to a fancy dinner, and one of the guests thinks he's pretty important, so he sits at the head of the table.

C1: And then the host makes him get up and move down to the foot.

C2: We think what you are doing is kind of risky.

A: Oh, no, I don't really think it is the same at all. It's just something we're doing to try and be helpful.

T: Yes, don't you worry about it. Go along and sit down again. Everything is quite all right. Just go back and sit down (*Makes shooing motions*).

(*The two children look at each other, shrug, and return to their seats.*)

A: Well, back to work, Theophilus. Where were we? (*T is watching the children leave and thinking hard.*) Theophilus?

T: You know, Amadeus, I'm just wondering . . .

A: Wondering what?

T: Well, wondering if maybe those children are right.

A: What do you mean?

T: Well, it *is* God's party.

A: Well, I know that.

T: And now they've got me thinking about that verse in Romans.

A: Which verse in Romans? There are a lot of them, you know.

T: Romans 15:7. "Welcome one another, therefore, just as Christ has welcomed you, for the glory of God."

A: (*Taps nose thoughtfully with pen and then very carefully sets it and pad down*) Hey, you two. Could you come back up here? (*The children return.*)

T: I think we need to do a little discerning here.

A: Yeah, do you really think we are doing the wrong thing here?
(*The two children look at each other and then nod vigorously.*)

T: (*Sighs*) Well, you know, we think maybe you're right.

A: So I guess we'd better stop. Do you think God will forgive us?

C1: Have you asked God?

A and T: (*Look at each other, then squeeze their eyes shut, fold their hands together*) Dear God, we're sorry and we won't do it again.

C2: There, now it's all right (*Pats nearest fool on arm and then the two sit down again*).

T: (*Clearing throat*) So, Amadeus, what's the word for today?

A: *The people of God*, Theophilus. All those people like us who are pilgrims on a journey, trying to respond to God's invitation.

T: All those people like us, who stumble along and sometimes goof up.

A: All those people like us, who do the best they can, discerning together and forgiving each other and, with the grace of God, slowly finding their way.

T: Well, Amadeus, time to get on the road.

A: Time to keep traveling. And the rest of you—don't forget, there's joy in the journey.

T: And we're all in this together. So God bless!

A: And see you at the party!

CHAPTER 5

The People of God

THE NEW COMMUNITY

God keeps reaching out to the world, offering love, mercy, and restored relationship. The people that respond to God's call are not like the haphazard group that collects at the jangling sound of the ice-cream truck's music, buying their cones and then wandering off again. We respond to God's call and are built by the Holy Spirit into a new creation. We become a new people, a new community whose character is modeled after the character of God, a holy nation. We are called out, not to be superior, but to be a light to the world. We become a holy priesthood who offer to God the sacrifice of transformed lives and a transformed community. We become the royal priesthood who sing God's song and who praise God in word and deed.

Come to him, a living stone,
> though rejected by mortals
> yet chosen and precious in God's sight,
> and like living stones,
>> let yourselves be built into a spiritual house,
>> to be a holy priesthood,
>> to offer spiritual sacrifices
>>> acceptable to God through Jesus Christ . . .

> . . . you are a chosen race,
> a royal priesthood,
> a holy nation,
> God's own people,

in order that you may proclaim
the mighty acts of him who called you
out of darkness into his marvelous light.

Once you were not a people,
but now you are God's people;
once you had not received mercy,
but now you have received mercy (1 Peter 2:4–5, 9).

We have been called to a great celebration, and we have come. We come, but sometimes we find ourselves rather taken aback by the other guests who have shown up. It is a motley crowd that God is gathering together, a company of surprises.

Jesus told a story about a great banquet. The host planned a great feast, and he sent out invitations well in advance so his guests could get it on their calendars. The time came and his household was busy for days, cleaning and baking and getting things ready. On the day itself the meat was roasting and the final preparations were well in hand, so the host sent his servant around to all the bigwigs in the town to tell them it was time to come. But they were all busy and sent their regrets. The host was ready to party, and he wasn't going to be stopped by a little thing like his invited guests not showing up. So he told his servant to go out and bring in all the street people and beggars. They came gladly, but there was still plenty of space and plenty of food. So the host told his servant to go out to the surrounding countryside and to drag in everyone he met, because the host wanted his rooms to be bursting at the seams.

In our sometimes too tidy and homogenous congregations, we forget the complex reality that is the people of God. "This man welcomes tax-collectors and sinners and eats with them," the Pharisees grumbled about Jesus. The host gathers in all the street people and beggars and raggle-taggle gypsies. When we come to the celebration, we don't know whom we will find sitting beside us. But we are urged to "welcome one another, therefore, just as Christ has welcomed you, for the glory of God" (Romans 15:7). It is the Lord's Table we gather around, and we are all fellow guests.

THE WELCOMING CHRIST

Jesus Christ welcomes us to his table. I learned this in a new way a few years ago. I was waiting for the beginning of a children's choir festival sponsored by a regional conference of the Mennonite church. It was held in the gymnasium of a nearby high school. The bleachers were out on the wall across from the stage; the floor was covered with chairs and all were full of people. I was sitting near the top of the bleachers, looking out over the crowd. It was a gathering of mostly Mennonites, but Mennonites of all kinds. I noticed the different shades of hair, the old people and the young people, people from the cities and people from the country, fat people and skinny people, people with nose-rings and people with head-coverings. I looked out over all those people, and I saw among them friends whom I have known for 20 or 30 years. I saw former students and people from my congregation. I saw acquaintances and people I knew by reputation. And I saw many, many people whom I did not know at all.

I looked out over all these people and I thought about stories. I knew my own story, and I knew some stories of people I saw, bits and pieces of their lives. I looked around, and I saw people with stories of hope and stories of pain, stories of success and stories of failure, stories of abuses and stories of healings. I looked at those I didn't know and wondered about their stories. Spread out before me was a smorgasbord of story, so huge that I couldn't begin to grasp it.

Suddenly I had a strong sense of Christ being present, not visible, yet somehow there with outspread arms, looking over the whole gathering. While I had only little bits of knowing and assumptions about peoples' stories, beliefs, and backgrounds, Christ knew each one of us there, knew us through and through. He knew our personalities and our past experiences, our struggles and our temptations, our successes and our failures, the ways we've grown and the ways we have yet to grow. Not only did Christ know each one of us to our very depths, but at the same time he loved each one of us completely and was there, longing to gather us in, like a mother hen calling her chicks and folding them under her wings. A complete acceptance, yet with the knowledge that as we respond and accept that acceptance, Christ draws us further in and further up, to be transformed more fully into the likeness of Christ.

Anne Lamott writes in *Traveling Mercies*, "God loves us exactly the way we are, and God loves us too much to let us stay like this." Anne is one of those guests that many of our staid, respectable congregations would be astonished to find in their midst. In the middle of a life that was messed up with alcoholism, bulimia, drugs, sex, and broken relationships, but that also had traces of God at work, she found her way into tiny ramshackle St. Andrews Presbyterian, drawn by the gospel music drifting out into the dusty alleys of the ethnic flea market she loved to visit. There she found "a choir of five black women and one rather Amish-looking white man making all that glorious music, and a congregation of thirty people or so, radiating kindness and warmth." Stiff, cautious, ready to bolt at an ill-considered question, she found herself coming back again and again, first standing at the door and then taking a seat at the back, but always leaving before the sermon because Jesus made about as much sense as Scientology or dowsing to her. The singing drew her in and captured her, wearing down the boundaries and distinctions that kept her isolated. "Sitting there, standing with them to sing, sometimes so shaky and sick that I felt like I might tip over, I felt bigger than myself, like I was being taken care of, tricked into coming back to life. But I had to leave before the sermon."

Then came the time when she was recovering from an abortion, sick and hungover, and she became aware of a strong presence watching her with patience and love, and she knew it was Jesus. She turned her back on this utterly impossible presence, but throughout the following week she had the feeling that a little stray cat was following her, wanting her to notice it and to let it in. She resolutely said, "No, I would rather die."

And one week later, when I went back to church, I was so hungover that I couldn't stand up for the songs, and this time I stayed for the sermon, which I just thought was so ridiculous, like someone trying to convince me of the existence of extraterrestrials, but the last song was so deep and raw and pure that I could not escape. It was as if the people were singing in between the notes, weeping and joyful at the same time, and I felt like their voices or *something* was rocking me in its bosom, holding me like a scared kid, and I opened up to that feeling—and it washed over me.[1]

She began to cry and left before the benediction, racing home, feeling that little stray cat at her heels. She stood at the door to her home, swore, and then took a deep breath and said, "All right. You can come in." She said yes to Christ.

Reading Anne's story, I had to acknowledge that while she could well have been drawn into my congregation by our singing, I don't know if we would have shown her the same grace and acceptance that St. Andrews did. We might not have known what to do with her language, or her fears, or her lifestyle. But we don't get to pick and choose who the other guests are. Christ sought out Anne and welcomed her in; can we do any less? Anne's book is a collection of essays on her life and the ways that God is welcoming her in and helping her to change. It is not an abrupt transformation, but a slow healing that takes effort and saying again and again, "All right. You can come in."

Anne's story may be more dramatic, but it is no different in nature than any of the rest of the company of Christians. We are a company of imperfect people, with stories of hope and failure, welcomed by Christ and being transformed by the Holy Spirit. We may long to be the church without spot or wrinkle, pure and holy and without blemish, but we have not yet come to the moment of that end-times vision. For now, like Paul, we have not yet reached the goal, but we press on. As we sing in the song, "We are pilgrims on a journey, we are trav'lers on the road. We are here to help each other walk the mile and bear the load."

Pause for reflection

♪ *How has Christ been at work in your life,
transforming sin and brokenness?*

♪ *In what ways does your congregation welcome
imperfect pilgrims?*

UNITY IN DIVERSITY

In her novel for youth, A *Wrinkle in Time*, Madeleine L'Engle paints a dismal portrait of a place where uniformity is valued over diversity. Her young protagonists land on the planet Camazotz and discover a town that is not unlike their own. Only here everything is laid out with mathematical exactness, in harsh angular patterns. All the houses are gray boxes, exactly alike. Each has a rectangular lawn, with a row of dull-looking flowers edging the path to the door. L'Engle's heroine, Meg, has the feeling that if she could count the flowers, there would be exactly the same number for each house.

Meg and her friends discover that here all the children play exactly the same thing at exactly the same moment; they even bounce their balls at exactly the same second. The adults' lives are equally carefully regulated and calibrated by IT, the giant, cold brain. No deviations are tolerated. This is uniformity in the extreme.

In contrast, Paul told the Corinthians that the church is like a living, breathing body, with its many parts. Here is diversity held in unity, not uniformity:

Indeed, the body does not consist of one member but of many.
If the foot would say,
   "Because I am not a hand, I do not belong to the body,"
      that would not make it any less a part of the body.
And if the ear would say,
   "Because I am not an eye, I do not belong to the body,"
      that would not make it any less a part of the body.
If the whole body were an eye, where would the hearing be?
If the whole body were hearing, where would the sense of smell be?
   But as it is, God arranged the members in the body,
      each one of them, as he chose.
If all were a single member, where would the body be?
   As it is, there are many members, yet one body.
The eye cannot say to the hand, "I have no need of you,"
nor again the head to the feet, "I have no need of you"
(1 Corinthians 12:14–23).

We Christians are a living body, a unity of diverse parts. Each of us comes as a unique child of God, with our own particular personality, our own portmanteau of experiences, our own ways of seeing, learning styles, approaches to conflict, and ways of interacting with others. We are not all the same and this is the way God intended it to be. We bring this unique combination of seeing and being to our congregational discernment. You, from your perspective, may have insights or questions that never would have occurred to me. I may have ideas that you would never have thought of. Together we are able to consider more than we could apart.

The goal of congregational discernment is to move toward this unified diversity, rather than uniformity or unanimity. Quakers, drawing on centuries of experience in congregational discernment, are sensitive to this distinction. They shake their heads over assumptions that the Quaker approach to decision making means that all decisions are unanimous, with everyone in full agreement. They are even somewhat uncomfortable with talk of consensus, finding that it doesn't quite capture the Quaker idea of seeking unity. Michael J. Sheeran uses a musical metaphor to describe this unity: ". . . the sort of agreement found in Quaker decisions is not an identity of view such that every participant ends up on the same note. Instead, they remain on different notes but blend them as the pianist blends complementary notes into a chord."[2]

Our diversity is a gift. It is through diversity that the Body is built up. Just before and just after the vivid imagery of the Body of Christ, Paul talks about the many different gifts of the Spirit, all of which have a role to play in the functioning of the Body. Our diversity is a gift from God, given that we may care for each other and help one another grow into mature faith. It is no accident that Paul, after speaking about our diverse gifts, launches in to his great hymn to Love, the "still more excellent way." Our diversity, rooted in love, helps the Body to grow into the fullness of Christ.

We are to welcome one another in our diversity, seeking unity in our discernment, not conformity or uniformity. God is not expecting us to all look and act and think exactly like each other. We are, however, called to be one—one with each other, one with Christ Jesus, and one with God. Paul wrote to the Philippians, urging them to be of the same mind and the same love that was in Christ Jesus. He didn't mean that they should all think the same thoughts. He wanted them to have the same approach to life as Christ did, the same attitude of setting self aside, the same love for one another. We are called to a unity of living our lives in a manner worthy of the gospel of Christ. We are called to a unity of love.

Pause for reflection

  ◈ *In what ways is your congregation uniform?*

  ◈ *In what ways does your congregation show a unified diversity?*

HEALTHY CONFLICT

Diversity is a gift. Hand-in-hand with diversity come disagreements. Disagreements happen as we brush up against the differences inherent in our diversity. We often are not ready to welcome these disagreements as a gift. We pull back. We assume that the others are not listening properly or have not understood—otherwise, surely they would see things just like we do. Some of us carry scars of past bitter quarrels or nasty church divisions. We know what rampant conflict can do and we do not want to go there.

But conflict can also be a gift. Disagreement creates an opportunity for transformation. In his book, *Journey Toward Reconciliation*, John Paul Lederach explores how we can turn conflict into life-giving encounter. Facing our conflict, engaging with those who disagree with us, we discover an opportunity for encounter—encounter with ourselves, with each other, and with God. Such encounter can be painful, but it can also bring life. We do not find the route to unity by ignoring or smoothing over our disagreement. We come to unity through facing and engaging our differences, with the help of the Holy Spirit.

Lederach draws on his years of experience working with conflict situations around the world as he reflects on biblical passages that speak to how the new community of God's people is to handle conflict. His discussions of Matthew 18:15–17 and Acts 15, which I have combined and condensed below, give us insight into healthy conflict.

Recognize and address conflict. When we bump up against a problem with a sister or brother in the church, we should go directly to them, rather than gossiping with friends about what so-and-so did or said. At a congregational level, we should address a conflict that is brewing, rather than trying to ignore it or sweep it under the rug.

Create appropriate forums and processes for addressing conflict. Some conflict should be dealt with one-on-one; at other times, conflict should be worked with in a small group, at a congregational level, or even more broadly (as when Antioch and Jerusalem believers met together in Acts 15). Whatever the setting, cultivate an atmosphere that supports the skills and spiritual disciplines that help transform conflict. Remember that our ultimate goal is restoration and reconciliation.

Develop and use skills that aid conflict transformation.
- When going directly, do so with "heart in hand," open to true engagement with the other, rather than defensively or confrontationally.
- Be clear about who you yourself are, engage non-anxiously with others, and maintain emotional and relational contact even when disagreeing.
- Learn to speak well and listen carefully, in both one-on-one encounters and in the congregational setting.
- Provide space for the open expression of diverse viewpoints.
- Develop the skill of "active listening": listening and responding to another person in such a way that they know you have heard and understood what they said.
- Use the many different gifts in the community—we each bring different strengths and skills that can contribute to our discernment.

Practice spiritual disciplines. Lederach suggests four:
- *Prayerful vulnerability.* Prayerful vulnerability calls for holding myself open to God and to the other, coming with a stance of listening, ready to learn about myself and my fears, instead of defending myself or arguing my own position.
- *Responsible discernment.* Responsible discernment refers to the role of the church in discerning what sin is. Responsible discernment

also calls for me to be aware of when addressing the other is appropriately mine to do—not letting slip what shouldn't, nor feeling responsible for carrying the whole world on my shoulders.

• *Interactive engagement.* Interactive engagement calls for me to approach my brother or sister, ready to share transparently and to interact constructively with the experiences, views, and differences that emerge as we talk and listen.

• *Prophetic listening.* Prophetic listening is a prayerful listening to God and to the other. It is "the discipline of listening with others in such a way that it helps them get in touch with what God is telling them."[3]

Decide, then implement decisions. Bring closure to the process—find a conclusion. Process is important, but not endless. In Acts, the group finds a way to welcome the new while holding on to some of the important past. In Matthew, the one who refuses to listen to the church is to be treated as a Gentile and a tax collector. While this is often taken as a mandate to end the relationship, Lederach reminds us that the movement of each of the steps in Matthew 18 is toward restoration and reconciliation. Jesus chose to eat with Gentiles, tax collectors, Pharisees, and fishermen. If we follow in Jesus' footsteps, we will maintain relationship even when we deeply disagree.

Disagreements are a natural part of congregational discernment. We can welcome healthy conflict as a sign of life and an opportunity for new growth. Indeed, some chaos, confusion, and conflict are to be expected in discernment. Agreement that comes too easily may be a sign of groupthink or blind custom. We can develop the disciplines and the skills that allow us to move through conflict, rather than allowing it to degenerate into a battle that tears us apart. Disagreement is a necessary part of the journey of discernment.

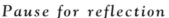

Pause for reflection

❧ *What is your normal reaction to conflict? Do you provoke it? Avoid it? Address it reluctantly? Embrace it?*

❧ *How are you growing in your response to conflict?*

♪ *How does your congregation typically react to conflict? Is there a current conflict in your congregation that comes to mind? How does this section shape your understanding of that conflict?*

THE FORGIVING COMMUNITY

As a community of imperfect pilgrims working through our conflict, we are called to be a discerning community. We are to sort out what is consistent with the character of God and what is not, and so clothe ourselves with Christ. We are also called to be a forgiving community, treating each other with gentleness and speaking truth in love. Being discerning and being forgiving are intrinsic to the character of the new community called into existence by God.

Caught up in the exuberant, overflowing excitement of Luke's account of Pentecost, we often overlook a much quieter story of the gift of the Holy Spirit. In John 20, it is the evening of the first day of the week after Jesus' crucifixion. The disciples are huddled together behind locked doors. It is a far cry from the joyous Easter morning services we are accustomed to celebrating. The disciples are fearful and confused, unsure of what the authorities might be about to do or what they themselves should be doing. That morning Peter and another disciple had come running in with a story about an empty tomb, and Mary Magdalene had an even more bewildering story about actually seeing and talking with Jesus.

The room is buzzing with questions and uncertainties and half-hearted proposals. Then suddenly Jesus is there in their midst, greeting them with the ordinary, everyday greeting, "Peace be with you." When the crescendo of astonishment dies down, Jesus gives them his commission, saying again, but with deeper significance, "Peace be with you," and then continues, "As the Father has sent me, so I send you." Then just as God the Creator bestowed the gift of the breath of life on newly formed humanity, Jesus breathes on his disciples, giving them the Holy Spirit. And he goes on, saying, "Receive the Holy Spirit. If you forgive the sins of any, they are forgiven them; if you retain the sins of any, they are retained." He sends his disciples out into the world with the responsibility of being both discerning and forgiving.

This same responsibility shows up in Matthew, though in slightly different language. In Matthew 16, Jesus tells Peter that whatever he binds on earth will be bound in heaven, and whatever he looses on earth will be loosed in heaven. In Matthew 18, this same language is used about the *ekklēsia*, the church. This phrase, "binding and loosing," is a rabbinical term. Jews came to the rabbis with problem cases and questions about how scriptural commandments were to be applied in contemporary settings. Moral teaching and decision making took the form of rulings on these problem cases. The rabbis might "bind," ruling something as either obligatory or forbidden, or they might "loose," ruling it instead as being left free, permissible. Jesus is giving the church the authority to make these types of discerning rulings—not just the church leadership, but the whole assembly.

In addition, the verse about binding and loosing comes in the middle of teachings on forgiveness. Matthew placed the parable of the shepherd and his search for the one strayed sheep just before the teaching on how the church is to respond to sin. Just after it he placed Peter's question about how often he should forgive someone who has sinned against him. "Seven times?" Peter generously suggests and Jesus answers, "Not just seven times, but seventy times seven," and goes on to tell the parable of the unforgiving servant. The parallel texts in John 20 (given above) and Luke 17:3–4 ("If another disciple sins, you must rebuke the offender, and if there is repentance, you must forgive") reiterate that discernment is closely connected with forgiveness.

Being discerning and being forgiving are closely interwoven. Forgiveness has no meaning without awareness that there are some actions that are wrong, actions for which one needs forgiveness. We must be discerning, identifying what is sinful and incompatible with God. There *is* sin and we *do* fall short of the glory of God. Sometimes we know that we have done wrong; at other times our sharply honed skills of rationalization snap into action and we don't recognize our own separation from God. Therefore, there is a need for mutual admonition within the faith community, the giving and receiving of counsel, speaking truth in love.

It is not easy to know how to do this. Some modern tendencies get in our way. On one side there is the problem of individualism. When we assume that what we do is our own business only and no one else has any right to speak to it, when we hesitate to address others because what they do is their own decision and they aren't harming others, then we will be neither discerning nor forgiving. It is tolerance, perhaps, but a tolerance that is in some essential way unconnected with the other, unconcerned with the other's welfare. It ignores the call to speak the truth in love, and to gently restore one who falls into sin.

On the other side, there is the problem of legalism. When we assume the rules can be understood in only one possible way and that there is no need for discernment, we may read Matthew 18 with a "1-2-3, y'er out" approach, losing sight of the individual. It is obedience, perhaps, but an obedience that again is in some essential way unconnected with the other, unconcerned with the other's welfare. It ignores the parable about motes and logs, and Jesus' words about coming not for the healed but for the sinners.

As Jesus illustrated with the parable of the unforgiving servant, our address of each other must be consistent with the character of God. It must be based solidly on a foundation of love for one another and willingness to forgive one another. We are not to judge in the sense of handing down a sentence, but we are to judge in the sense of determining what is incompatible with God. Our task is not to keep the church pure, but to help each other move out of sinful behavior and to grow in Christlikeness, restoring right relationship with God and with the community. Our focus is to be on building up the Body and helping one another bear each other's burdens, knowing that the one who corrects may another day be the one who is corrected. In learning to live as a forgiven and forgiving community, we join in God's vision for a world that is reconciled with God, with each other, and with all creation.

Pause for reflection

❦ *Does your congregation practice mutual admonition? How does it do so?*

❦ *In what ways do you, and your congregation, live as a forgiven and forgiving people?*

THE DISCERNING COMMUNITY

The new community of God's people is called to be a welcoming, discerning, healing community. Its congregational discernment is multi-faceted, speaking to many different kinds of decisions. For the Anabaptist-Mennonite tradition, one important facet of discernment has been asking questions about how we live our lives faithfully. Ethical decisions and mutual admonition have been part of the way we have understood the call to be a discerning community. This is a strand that often receives less emphasis in contemporary writings on congregational discernment. It is a challenging strand. In addition to carrying an awareness of the importance of this facet of discernment, Anabaptist-Mennonites carry a heavy tradition of many splits and divisions caused by disagreement about what it means to live faithfully. Nonetheless, this ethical discernment is a crucial strand as we seek to offer the praise of our words and deeds to God. It is vital that we develop healthy ways of working at conflict, of finding creative ways to live in the tension of being a welcoming, discerning, forgiving community.

In Romans, Paul writes about some of the struggles and disagreements the Roman churches were facing. They were wrestling with different understandings of whether some days should be seen as holy, and of what sorts of food it was acceptable to eat. Paul urges them not to pass judgment on one another, but instead to do all they can to build one another up. He encourages them to come to unity, so that they might give glory to God. "May the God of steadfastness and encouragement grant you to live in harmony with one another, in accordance with Christ Jesus, so that together you may with one voice glorify the God and Father of our Lord Jesus Christ" (Romans 15:5–6).

Reading on in verse 7, Paul encourages us to "Welcome one another, therefore, just as Christ has welcomed you, for the glory of God." We are to welcome one another in all our diversity, working through our disagreements, and growing into the new community in Christ. As the Body of Christ, we are not left to our own feeble efforts. Jesus does not simply give us the authority to bind and loose. He promises his presence and his aid. Matthew 18 closes with his words, "Again, truly I tell you, if two of you agree on earth about anything you ask, it will be done for you by my Father in heaven. For where two or three are gathered in my name, I am there among them." Gathered in his name, we are co-workers in Christ's ministry of reconciliation, discerning God's song together.

> So if anyone is in Christ,
>   there is a new creation:
> everything old has passed away;
>   see, everything has become new!
> All this is from God,
>   who reconciled us to himself through Christ,
> and has given us the ministry of reconciliation;
>
> that is, in Christ God was reconciling the world to himself,
>   not counting their trespasses against them,
> and entrusting the message of reconciliation to us
> (2 Corinthians 5:17–20).

NOTES

[1] Anne Lamott, *Traveling Mercies: Some Thoughts on Faith*. (New York: Pantheon Books, 1999), 44–50, 135.

[2] Michael J. Sheeran, S.J. *Beyond Majority Rule: Voteless Decisions in the Religious Society of Friends*. (Philadelphia: Philadelphia Yearly Meeting, 1983), 64.

[3] John Paul Lederach, *The Journey Toward Reconciliation*. (Scottdale: Herald Press, 1999), 155.

Process

Note: This dialogue is more complicated than the others, but it has been done! Prepare props and practice with song leader ahead of time. You may want to cue "volunteers" ahead of time.

Additional readers: Song leader, volunteers to play rhythm instruments

Props:
- mat (or cardboard) with rectangle cut out of center
- bag of instruments attached by string to protractor
- a conductor's baton
- a pitch pipe
- rhythm instruments, each with one of these labels: "an interpretation of Scripture," "a personal story," "a financial figure," "a theological understanding," "a cultural framework," "a congregational experience," "a Mennonite perspective"

T: Hi! I'm Theophilus.

A: And I'm Amadeus.

T: We're pilgrims on a journey.

A: Two fools for Christ who wander the world,

T: trying to put into words what can't be put into words,

A: trying to understand mystery and paradox and talk about them with people like you.

T: So what's the word for today, Amadeus?

A: The word for today, Theophilus, is . . . (*Almost inaudibly, to side*) *process.*

T: What was that?

A: (*Wincing in anticipation*) Umm, *process.*

T: Process? Oh, no, not *process.*

A: Hey, don't blame me. It's their idea.

T: Their idea?

A: Well, okay, maybe not all of them—I've heard a rumor that some of them get really irritated by the word *process,* too.

T: Well, I sure don't blame them. Process, process, process. All that means is talk, talk, talk, and then in the end all you've got is processed cheese.

A: Processed *cheese*?

T: You know, that soft orange stuff that comes in little flat squares wrapped in plastic, and is all bland, and gooey, and sticks to the roof of your mouth.

A: Oh, great. Now you've ruined the word for me, too (*Reflects*). Okay, look. Forget the word *process*. What they really want us to talk about is how you *do* discernment.

T: You mean we're finally getting down to some nitty-gritty practical stuff?

A: Guess so.

T: Well, it's about time. Let's go for it! (*all set to dig in, then confused*) Umm, Amadeus? What *is* the practical stuff?

A: You mean, how do we actually do discernment?

T: Yeah, where do we start? What do we do?

A: Well, we . . . um . . . we . . . how come you get to ask all the questions today?

T: You're not sure how to do it either, are you? (*A shakes head "no."*) Well, okay. No need to panic. Let's put on our thinking caps and see if we can come up with anything (*They straighten their fools' caps and reflect*).

A: Okay, I've got an idea. But I think it is going to set you off again.

T: (*Outraged innocence*) Who, me? Why?

A: Because in order to do discernment together, we have to talk (*T with a deep sigh, roll of eyes*). Now just wait. It's got to be a special kind of talking. A special kind of talking and *listening*. We don't want processed cheese. We want to end up with a powerful song that is in tune with God's song.

T: So what kind of talking is that—an operetta?

A: Look, are you going to help me here or not?

T: Okay, okay. So what's the question?

A: I think what they really want to know is how to talk together so that they get somewhere with their discernment, and don't just spin their wheels.

T: Makes sense to me—who wants to be a gerbil?

A: So, you got any ideas?

T: Maybe we can find something in here (*Sets kit sack on table*).

A: So, what's in it? We can use all the help we can get (*They open sack and begin looking at tools*).

T: You know, there are some really strange tools in here.

A: What's this? (*Holds up mat with rectangle cut out of middle*)

T: (*Takes it and tries framing different views*) It reminds me of something I once saw an artist using to frame a view.

A: (*Peers through it at view, nods, then notices*) Hey, look—there's some writing on it.

T: (*Reading*) "First frame the question." Frame the question?

A: Hey! That's what we've just been doing! You know, trying to figure out what we're really supposed to talk about here. What have you got there?

T: (*Holds up protractor*) This says it's for looking at the question from many different angles (*String attaches protractor to bag in sack*).

A: Look, Theophilus, it's connected to this bag. *(Pulls out bag of rhythm instruments: triangle, maracas, etc. As T and A pull out instruments, they read the labels.)* That's sure a lot of angles, Theo.

T: Angles, instruments—whatever. *(Looks to congregation)* Shall we try them out? Can we have some helpers up here? *(Hands an instrument to each volunteer, has them line up beside table)*

A: Okay! Go for it! *(Everybody plays at once, making utter chaos)*

T & A: Wait! Wait! Stop! Hold it! *(Music makers stop)*

A: Boy, that was awful!

T: Yeah, it sounded exactly like some congregational meetings I've been to. Is there anything in that sack that can help?

A: What about this? *(Holds up conductor's baton)* Does anyone know how to use one of these?

Song leader: *(Coming forward)* I can give it a try. I think it will help if everyone doesn't try to play at once. *(Gestures with baton to invite one instrument to play and then signals for them to stop, goes on to next and so on)*

A: Well, that's more orderly. But it's kind of boring.

Song leader: So maybe we need to see if we can work together a bit more. Here, how about if you start us off with a beat? *(With baton and voice, gets all the instruments playing together with different but co-ordinated rhythms and then signals for them to stop)*

T: Well, that's better. At least you are playing *with* each other and the song leader now.

A: It still feels to me like something is missing, though.

T: Maybe we need to add this (*Holds up pitch pipe and blows note*).

Song leader: *(Invites everyone in class/congregation to join in singing a simple, repeated word on the pitch such as "Gloria" or "Alleluia" and then brings the rhythm instruments in as well, then stops it)*

T: Hey, we're really starting to make music together here! Thank you, all you volunteers.

A: Yes, you can go sit down again. (*To T*) So what does that pitch pipe have written on it?

T: "The Holy Spirit in the midst of the gathered congregation." Wow.

A: Yeah. I just wish it were always as easy to hear the Holy Spirit as it is to hear that pitch pipe.

T: We're running out of time. Is there anything else in that kit sack we should mention?

A: I just found a whole bunch more! (*T and A poke around in sack without lifting things out and take turns calling out what they are finding—"Here's something that says 'Five Minute Silence.'" "This says 'Five Finger Tool.'" "Examine the cons and pros." "Testing an option." "Group Lectio Divina")* And there's still more in here.

T: More than we can talk about right now, it looks like.

A: I'm afraid so. But at least we've made a start. Maybe this group can talk about the tools later.

T: Thanks to all of you for joining in and helping us make music (*Gathers up instruments, while A packs other tools back in kit sack, and they leave*).

CHAPTER 6

The Creative Play of Discernment

When our two children were much younger, they had a favorite baby-sitter, Reid, who enjoyed helping them put together elaborate creations. His arrival was the signal for the children to pull out the three sets of building blocks, the train set, and all the stuffed animals. As we left, the three of them would be earnestly discussing what they should build that evening. While we were gone, they built, revised, came up with bright ideas, and revised again. One of them might propose adding a treasure room to the palace they were creating for the stuffed elephant and cat dynasties, and another would think of getting the dress-up necklaces for treasure, and then the other would run upstairs for dessert bowls to be used as crystal treasure containers.

Sometimes ideas clashed and a squabble would develop. Then Reid would help them sort it out and refocus on their project once more. Sometimes the squabble would continue and grow, and then Reid would have to call an end to the project and they would put everything away. But more frequently we would arrive at home to find them happily playing with a completed palace, or a town and train layout that filled the family room, or a child-high maze of blocks. They would eagerly point out the highlights of the palace, or show us how the train could successfully navigate around the room, or demonstrate that if you put a marble *here*, it would roll *there*—the maze of blocks was actually a functioning marble roller.

The creative process they went through in building these wonders had several phases: getting out the toys they needed, deciding what to build, putting together their creation, testing it, and putting it to use. The details of what they did in each phase varied, depending on the project, but the basic outline remained the same. In the same way, we can talk about the basic phases of the creative process of discernment.

Just as the children's creations were unique, each time of congregational discernment is also unique. How we go about discernment together is shaped in part by the question asked. Deciding whether to renovate or build new worship space will not involve the same details as choosing a new pastor. Listening for the ways a congregation is being called to new vision and mission will not proceed along the same lines as determining how to respond to ethical ambiguities. Yet, while the details differ, underneath the variation is a basic framework. There are phases in congregational discernment, just as with the children's creative play: preparation, gathering information, discussion, decision, and implementing our decision.

Congregational discernment is aided by our awareness that there are different phases with different tasks. Having a sense of where we are in the process helps us to work together rather than at cross-purposes. These phases are outlined below, but anyone who has participated in congregational discernment will quickly recognize that these are broad brush-strokes. This outline is a simple version. Its phases move smoothly in linear progression. To be sure, sometimes our discernment does happen this simply. We zip through the middle steps in fifteen minutes at a congregational meeting. At other times, though, it is more complicated. Some decisions may require multiple meetings, spread over many months. Sometimes we find we need to return to earlier phases, realizing that we are missing needed information, or that our task is not clear, or that the query needs to be clarified. Sometimes we realize that our disagreement is becoming more intense. We may need to call in outside help, or even lay our attempt at discernment aside for a time. This does not mean that discernment doesn't work. As with other areas of congregational life, we do the best we can, asking for God's guidance and the Spirit's help.

PREPARATION

Before a query can be taken to the congregation for discernment, some preliminary work needs to be done. Just as the children had to decide whether to work on a palace or a marble roller, someone needs to decide what questions get taken to the congregation as a whole. The life of a congregation calls for many decisions; not all of these can, nor should, be brought for congregational discernment. Trying to deal with all of them as a group soon leads to getting bogged down in a mucky morass of trivia, which in turn leads to burnout and disinterest. Most congregations instead delegate routine matters to an appropriate committee or individual and ask the leadership group to discern which queries should come to the congregation as a whole. In chapter two we saw how wide-ranging these can be—choice of leadership, ethical issues, decisions about the character and activities of the congregation, calls to mission and service.

Congregational discernment begins with the leadership group doing its own work of discernment, prioritizing what questions are to come to the congregation and when. Once they determine the query, they focus it, framing it as clearly as they can at this point, while being aware that further clarification may come as the congregation works together. They also do some planning, deciding on the appropriate approach for this particular time of discernment.

Pause for reflection

✦ *What decisions has your congregation made recently? Who made the decision? The pastor? A leadership group? A committee? The congregation?*

✦ *What types of decisions come to the congregation as a whole? How is that determined?*

GATHERING INFORMATION

As with the children getting out their blocks and other toys, this second phase is the time for gathering and sharing the information the congregation needs for discernment, laying the bits and pieces out so that everyone knows what they are working with. The first step is the presentation of the query, along with whatever background information is helpful.

Those presenting should also be clear about what they are asking the congregation to do. Is this a query that calls for wide-open brainstorming? Does it involve the evaluation of particular options? Has a specific proposal been brought, and if so, does the leadership group assume that discussion will lead to modifications, or are they looking for a yes/no response? Is this a query that calls for study and reflection? Whatever the details of the approach to this particular query, the leadership group presents it as clearly as possible and allows time for questions of clarification about both query and task.

The next step is to share information. Different ones in the congregation carry pieces that need to become part of the congregational conversation. This involves both head and heart information—facts and figures, as well as insights, concerns, and stories of the way the Spirit has moved in our lives in connection with this query. When my congregation was considering renovating our building, we collected information about facts and figures: we consulted with an architect and with builders, explored options, and discussed costs. We also shared stories of the movement of the Spirit in our congregational life: the original decision to purchase a former factory and the hours of volunteer labor that went into that renovation; the decision to open our worship space to the kindergarten class of a nearby daycare center; and the fire that destroyed that center and our commitment to rebuild so that the whole center could be housed in our building. We heard stories from individuals and reflected on our values. One couple had recently returned from several years of working with churches in the Philippines, and they carried a strong awareness of the needs of churches in the developing world. Others of us also carried a strong concern for environmental effects and for good stewardship of both money and materials. Some of us carried a concern for aesthetics and the way the shape of the space affects worship. Each of these pieces, and more, needed to be laid out on the table so we could all be aware of them and carry them together.

The amount and type of information that is needed varies with the question being discerned. We look to Scripture, tradition, reason, experience, and more. Our discernment is grounded in Scripture interpreted through the guidance of the Holy Spirit in the community of faith, so a primary question we ask is what the scriptural conversation is in relation to our question. We learn from the church in other times and places—the stories and beliefs of our own faith tradition, as well as the insights and challenges coming from others. We give and receive coun-sel with other congregations and with denominational structures. We learn from science and technology, and we apply common sense. We bring our personal experiences—the whole web of personality, life expe-riences, and the ways God has been active in our lives. We examine the world around us, looking for those places where God is already at work. We examine our cultural setting and the ways the powers distort our vision—Zeus, Ares, Eros, and Hermes may no longer be worshiped as gods, but power, war, sexuality, and economics are still influential forces. The Holy Spirit may need to open our eyes to engrained ways of seeing the world that are in opposition to God's vision. Any of these areas may provide pieces that need to be shared in our congregational conversation.

Pause for reflection

𝕾 *Reflect on several recent congregational decisions. How was the question presented? Was it clear what the congregation was expected to do?*

𝕾 *What type of information was brought into the discussion?*

𝕾 *Did it include both head and heart information? What about the areas mentioned—Scripture, tradition, reason, experience, the powers, etc.?*

DISCUSSION

Building a marble roller or a block palace is creative play. There are no teams competing, no points scored, just children interacting together. At its best, discernment shares this same cooperative, playful charac-ter. In the discussion phase, we move from the initial presentation and clarifications to a more interactive discussion. Carrying the head and heart information it has gathered, the congregation begins to play with the pieces. The pieces do not just fit together like a puzzle, however. Our discussion is more of a creative process than that. We listen to each other, we test options, we build on others' suggestions with improvements, we explore disagreements, we weigh alternatives, and gradually we move toward discernment.

A special kind of interchange can develop, a mindful way of listening and speaking to each other. Disagreement is a natural part of this discussion, as we each speak from our own perspectives. Instead of listening to the other in search of weak points, or only half listening while preparing rebuttal comments, our focus is on facing our conflict and working through it to unity. We are a gathering of the body of Christ, seeking to know the heart and mind of God. Together we are listening for the Spirit's voice in our midst. We speak freely and listen attentively as others speak, because the Spirit may speak through any one of us.

We also listen for the Spirit in other ways. Quakers talk of conducting their meetings for business with the same expectant waiting for the guidance of the Spirit that they practice in meetings for worship. Their centered silence is one way of being attentive to God's presence. Other groups bring their own ways of worship. Song, prayer, guided Scripture meditations, and silence are all good paths into deepening our awareness of the One whose guidance we seek.

In his letters to the early churches, Paul repeatedly encourages his fellow believers to build each other up as they gather for worship and discernment. Maintaining an attentive, upbuilding, playful tone to our discernment is as much a matter of attitude as it is of technique. Attention to a number of dimensions can help keep the conversation cooperative and playful, even as we explore our disagreement.

- **Pace:** Rapid-fire exchanges leave little space for reflection or for active listening. We can encourage each other to slow down, and to finish listening to the one speaking before deciding what needs to be said next.
- **Styles:** People have different styles of learning and communicating. Some people thrive on speaking in large group settings and need little time to sort out what they want to say. Some need time for reflection before they are willing to speak, or prefer smaller settings. Some absorb information presented orally; some need to see it on a poster

or handout. We can plan for multiple ways of presenting and working with information in our discussion.

- **Intuition:** Incorporating art and music, metaphors and dreams, and interweaving our own story with the biblical Story expands our opportunities for hearing the Spirit. A timely metaphor can often do more than a spate of words to help people understand another point of view.

- **Power issues:** Power comes in many forms and can be used for good or for ill. We can raise our awareness of the temptations for negative use of power. Are age, race, education, wealth, gender, or other factors influencing whose voices are heard in our discussion? Are some voices dominating? Are some voices missing from our conversation? Some will need encouragement to speak; others need encouragement to listen; many, some of both.

Gradually the conversation draws toward a conclusion. Instead of the tentative testing of alternatives, comments begin to come together. We begin to get a sense that the marble roller is nearing completion. We are not looking for uniformity (all thinking alike), but for unity—the sense that together we have found the next step of the path to which God calls us. We may see signs that we are reaching a moment of discernment. The following are indicators, rather than infallible markers, but their presence can help us know when we are nearing a decision.

- **Charism of discernment:** 1 Corinthians 12 includes the discernment of spirits and the utterance of wisdom and of knowledge in its list of gifts of the Spirit. Over time, some among us will repeatedly show they have these gifts. Such people are not infallible, but we have learned to value their insights and questions. Are these "weighty members" (to use the Quaker phrase) in agreement? If they are not, we have probably not yet come to clarity. *Caution:* we can give undue weight to a person's words based on factors such as their wealth, gender, education, or years in the congregation, rather than on their insight or discernment. We should try to assess honestly why we are giving weight to someone's words.

- **Convergence:** People are drawn toward the same conclusion, but by different paths, for different reasons, or by drawing on different gifts. Or there is a convergence of apparently unrelated pieces within the group, or from the group's past, which unexpectedly come together—perhaps needed skills, or past experiences, or the synergy of several people interacting together.

- **Clarity:** The group as a whole feels a deep sense of rightness and clarity, rather than confusion and agitation.
- **Consistency with God's vision:** The decision the group appears to be reaching is in line with God's vision for justice, well-being, and right relationship. It remembers "the poor, the orphans, the widows and the strangers"—those on the margins.
- **Unity:** The group may have a sense of coming to a common mind after a period of exploration and disagreement. (If it comes before such a period, it may instead be a sign of groupthink or peer pressure.) This unity is especially significant when new ways of seeing are discovered and walls that have separated people are broken down.

Pause for reflection

❧ *What is the pace of the discussion in your congregational meetings?*

❧ *What styles of learning and communicating does the congregation use?*

❧ *How does the congregation value and draw on intuition?*

❧ *Do some voices dominate? Is there a pattern to who speaks and who is silent or is not present at the meeting?*

❧ *How does it leave space for the Holy Spirit?*

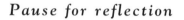

DECISION

The journey may be long and rocky, or it may be a short, pleasant stroll. Eventually we come to a moment of clarity and decision. We are able to declare that the marble roller is finished. Like the Jerusalem church described in Acts 15, we are able to say, "It seems good to the Holy Spirit and to us." Our discernment is done. In the decision phase, we come to this recognition and formally acknowledge it.

Most congregations have a customary way of finalizing decisions. For many, the details will be spelled out in their constitution or bylaws. The two most common ways of doing this in contemporary North American churches are through a vote or through reaching a consensus. Each has its own framework. Either can be an appropriate conclusion to a journey of discernment.

Congregations may also want to consider expanding their options for finalizing decisions. Some congregations are drawing on a number of different ways of making decisions, choosing the approach that is most appropriate for the query they are working on. This choice is made during the planning stage, before the congregational discussion begins, and is explicitly stated as the process begins. Consensus, voting, and modifications of these can all be good choices. Some possibilities to consider:

In a **pure consensus model**, we seek a conclusion to which all participants can give their consent. It does not mean uniformity, or an equal level of enthusiasm and agreement held by all. Some may continue to disagree with the decision, but choose to stand aside, allowing the group to move ahead. If, however, some continue to disagree and do not choose to stand aside, the decision is blocked, and the group will not go ahead with it. (See Appendix A, Part IV, B for the Spectrum of Dissent familiar to Quakers.)

In a **modified consensus model**, the congregation uses the same approach as in a pure consensus model, trying to discover a conclusion to which all can give their consent. But they also allow for the possibility of proceeding even if the group is blocked, agreeing before the discussion begins that they can move ahead on a vote passed by a specified majority (usually a significant percentage, such as 80 per cent).

Voting also has gradations: decisions can be made on the basis of a simple majority, or two-thirds, or three-quarters, or four-fifths, or another percentage. Important decisions will call for a higher percentage; others are adequately met by a simple majority vote. Voting can be done with a voiced aye/nay, a show of hands, or by written ballot. Ballots can be a straight yes or no, or can include the option of written explanations.

When the choice is between two or more equally good options, one possible response is to **cast lots**, as in Acts 1:26, where the disciples cast lots to choose the replacement for Judas. This approach is also familiar to Mennonites as a former way of choosing church leadership.

For some decisions, it may be appropriate to **count only the yes votes**. In their book, *Discerning God's Will Together*, Morris and Olsen describe a congregation that takes this approach under certain circumstances.[1] If they are considering a ministry or project that requires a certain number of volunteers, and the group as a whole approves the project, but doesn't want to vote on something others will need to carry out, they choose to count only the yes votes. Only those who are willing to actively carry out the project vote; if there are enough of these yes votes to carry out the project, the congregation goes ahead with it.

Pause for reflection

 How does your congregation acknowledge a moment of clarity and decision? What are the strengths of this method? The weaknesses?

 If you use a mixed approach, how do you determine when to use which method?

IMPLEMENTING OUR DECISION

Our discernment is done and our decision made, but the journey is not yet complete. When the children built a marble roller, they needed to test it by running a marble through it. Sometimes they thought they had finished, and then discovered a little tinkering was called for. Palaces might be completed, but the play wasn't over—the stuffed animals needed to be moved in and stories enacted. And the creations never really felt complete until they could be shared with us when we returned home.

Our congregational discernment is done, but it will not take us far unless we are committed to living it out. Someone needs to determine the details—who will do what by when—and then help the congregation to carry out the decision it made. Being clear about who that "someone" is can help us avoid situations where a decision is made or a study done, only to be put on a shelf and never looked at again. Who that "someone" is will vary depending on the decision. It may be the leadership group, the pastor, a standing committee, a specially named task force, or a gifted individual.

As we live into the decision, we may discover that it needs a little adjusting here and there. We may discover that we were off-base with our original discernment and need to take a step back. We may even have made the wrong decision. Or we may discover that the decision releases new energy and leads in directions we hadn't dreamed of. Taking time to evaluate our discernment and decisions is also an important phase of discernment. We can assess the results on a number of fronts:

Clarity: Is there a communal sense of rightness and clarity about what the group has decided, and a release of joy and energy that enables the group to carry out its decision? This is not the same as a sense of relief that a difficult discussion has ended.

Fruits of the Spirit: Are the fruits of the Spirit present? Are people treating each other with patience, kindness, and gentleness? Is there a sense of joy and peace growing out of the decision?

Fruitfulness: After time, we examine what happened as a result of the decision. Has it allowed us to grow in our relationship with God, or has it separated us? Did it produce fruit that is in line with God's heart for the poor, oppressed, and those on the margin? Is it moving us towards greater justice, well-being, and right relationships? A word of caution here: we need to allow sufficient time for the fruit to appear. We also need to examine whether we have done our share toward living out the decision.

Another aspect of evaluation comes in interaction with others. While decisions may be made congregationally, few congregations stand totally alone. We interact with other congregations in our community; we are part of regional and denominational structures. Some churches, such as the Catholic Church, have highly detailed expectations about what sort of decision is made where. Even those denominations with a strong tradition of congregationally based decision making will find themselves in conversation with others about the implications of some of their decisions. An important element of our discernment and of evaluating our decisions is giving and receiving counsel from others.

Pause for reflection

⸕ *What is your evaluation of the recent decisions you have looked at in the earlier questions? Did you find clarity? Has the outcome been fruitful? Have the fruits of the Spirit been evident?*

⸕ *Does your congregation have any customary ways of evaluating decisions that have been made?*

⸕ *How do you interact with the broader church in your decision making? In evaluation of the decisions?*

ROLE OF THE CONGREGATION

Discernment is a congregational activity. We come together to discern, just as we come together to worship. Good process helps us and good leadership enhances our discernment, but equally important are the attitudes we bring—attitudes toward ourselves, toward each other, and toward God.

Attitudes toward self

Bold humility: Each of us comes as a child of God, with our own unique combination of gifts, experiences, insights, and concerns. We each bring our own unique perspective on the query we are discerning, and we can speak boldly from that awareness. At the same time, we speak humbly, knowing that our own perspective is a partial one, and that others also bring facets that we need to hear.

Self-awareness: The more we become aware of our "built-in" tendencies, our knee-jerk responses, our strengths and weaknesses, the more we can learn to adjust for them and to manage them, instead of being controlled by them in discernment. This frees us to listen for the Spirit and opens us for transformation.

Spiritual formation: A commitment to our own personal spiritual growth—deepening our relationship with God, learning to watch for the ways God is active in our lives, spring-cleaning our cupboards—is an important contribution to our congregational discernment.

Attitudes toward others

Attentive listening: Remembering we each come with our own unique perspective, we listen carefully to each other. Others will bring insights, memories, or questions that never would have occurred to us. The Spirit can nudge or startle us into new awareness through the words of others, if we are paying attention.

Healthy conflict: Disagreements exist as a natural part of rubbing shoulders with others who see the world in their own way. We can treat conflict as an opportunity for growth, instead of smothering it or allowing it to tear us apart. Remembering that we each have blind spots, we can offer our perspective for the questions and testing of others, weighing and testing what they bring in turn.

Mutual care: A spirit of playful discernment is nurtured by our care for one another. All of us, not just those who facilitate the meeting, can tend to pace, style, and power issues. Our goal is to build up each individual and the community as a whole, speaking truth with love, carrying one another's burdens, and interacting with gentleness.

Attitudes toward God

Response to God: Discernment is our response to God, who loves us and who calls us to be the People of God. We want our words, actions, and decisions to be in tune with God, giving God glory and praise.

Expectant hope: We can enter discernment with the expectant hope that we will find our way together, even through difficult decisions. In the midst of our imperfections, blinders, and misunderstandings, the Spirit is at work to transform and guide us.

Faithful obedience: Some discernment traditions talk of "holy indifference"—the goal of being indifferent to all but what God desires. We can acknowledge our biases and preferences while also striving to hold them lightly, joining ourselves with Jesus' prayer: "Not my will but yours be done." Our discernment is not an end in itself, but is for the purpose of faithfully following Christ, sharing in God's mission in the world.

Presence of God: God is at the center of our discernment. We can interweave our discussions with prayer, song, silence, and other ways of focusing our attention on God's presence. We can nurture our congregational spiritual formation before and during times of discernment: worshipping together, building relationships with God and with each other, developing habits of attentive listening and truthful speaking, and learning to become wise readers of Scripture.

Pause for reflection

⟊ *What attitudes do you bring to congregational discernment and decision making? What attitudes does your congregation encourage?*

⟊ *How might you develop and strengthen attitudes that aid discernment?*

THE ROLE OF LEADERSHIP

Something special happened when Reid interacted with my children. Together they came up with more elaborate and interesting creations than when any one of them was alone. Reid didn't do it for them or direct their every step. Nor did he stand on the sidelines just watching. He was as involved in the play as the children were. They all contributed to the ideas and to the construction. But Reid's participation had an added dimension that enhanced their play. He helped keep them focused on what they were doing, encouraging them if their interest started to wane. He could function as a mediator, or even a referee, if need be. And more especially, he was someone the children trusted, someone with whom they enjoyed playing and who enjoyed playing with them.

This sort of participatory leadership is also an important element in discernment. For smaller groups, such leadership can happen informally. At the congregational level, it is helpful to designate leadership. Pastors, congregational leadership groups, and meeting facilitators each have a role to play. Congregations will vary in how these responsibilities are assigned; the important thing is that there be a clear understanding by both congregation and leadership of the expectations and responsibilities for the roles.

Leadership has ongoing responsibilities throughout discernment. Leaders can help keep the congregation focused on the goal of knowing and doing God's will. To do this, they themselves will want to maintain practices that keep them grounded and centered in God: prayer, Bible study, worship with the congregation, retreat time alone or as a group, interactions with a spiritual director.

Staying centered, they are able to provide a non-anxious presence and to connect with congregational participants. They are able to set the tone for discernment, reminding us of our goal of being in tune with God, helping us see the opportunities in conflict, calling us to be gentle with each other and to carry each other's burdens. They carry the congregation in their hearts, staying aware of overall group dynamics and knowing when special intervention may be needed. Such intervention can include pastoral care for those most affected by the congregational work, mediation in squabbles that are sidetracking the discernment, or providing guided retreats or prayer times in the midst of a difficult decision.

Through this grounded-ness and this awareness of the congregation, leaders can develop a sense of vision for the congregation, an opportunity that they sense God inviting the congregation to pick up. Or they may recognize such an opportunity in another's vision. Such visions are not imposed, but brought to the congregation for testing and discernment—for the kind of interactive play and creativity that went into building the children's marble rollers.

There are also specific responsibilities for leadership in the various phases of discernment. In preparation for discernment, designated leadership is responsible for discerning what is brought to the congregation as a whole, for framing the query as clearly as possible, and for planning the appropriate approach to a given question. In later phases, leading congregational meetings is an important role. The facilitator helps the congregation keep an eye on pace and power issues, and finds ways to include different styles and the use of intuition. He or she is familiar with the congregation's repertoire of discernment practices, and knows when to bring them into the discussion. He or she is also responsible for reading the meeting, having a sense of which phase the congregation is in, being able to put into words and test a possible discernment, and recognizing and naming when the congregation has indeed reached a moment of clarity.

In the final phase of living into and evaluating a decision, leadership enables the congregation to follow through with their response. Leaders help focus efforts, arrange for fine-tuning if needed, and lead the way in confession and change if it becomes clear that a wrong decision was made. They are a voice for the congregation, interacting with other congregations and denominational structures in giving and receiving counsel. They are also a voice within the congregation, encouraging and inspiring others as they too participate in living out the discernment reached together.

⸏⸏⸏

Pause for reflection

What are the expectations and responsibilities of leadership in your congregational decision making?

In what ways have leaders you have known set the tone for discernment? How have they helped discernment to happen?

⸏⸏⸏

NOTE
[1] Danny Morris & Charles Olsen, *Discerning God's Will Together: A Spiritual Practice for the Church* (Bethesda: Alban Publications, 1997), 135. On page 89, Morris and Olsen also discuss the idea of casting lots.

The Word

Additional readers: Older person from congregation

Props: Bible

T: Hi! I'm Theophilus.

A: And I'm Amadeus.

T: We're pilgrims on a journey.

A: Two fools for Christ who wander the world,

T: trying to put into words what can't be put into words,

A: trying to understand mystery and paradox and talk about them with people like you.

T: So, what's the word for today, Amadeus?

A: The word for today, Theophilus, is . . . *the Word.*

T: *The word* is the word?

A: Yes, the Word is the word for today.

T: This isn't one of those silly dialogues about who's on first, is it?

A: Not if I can help it.

T: Okay, so what do you mean, the word?

A: You know—Scripture, the Bible, the Holy Word.

T: Oh, the Bible. Why didn't you just say so?

A: Well, because the word they gave me was . . .

T: (*Interrupts*) See, I know the Bible. Back in grade school I was the star of our Sunday School Bible Drill Team. Go on—ask me anything.

A: Anything?

T: Anything from the Bible. Anything at all.

A: Okay, um . . . how many books are in the New Testament?

T: Oh, come on, everyone knows that! There are 27. Ask something hard.

A: Okay, um . . . what was the name of Moses' wife?

T: Oh, oh, I know that, I know that (*Hand raised, waving*). Just a minute, just a minute . . . it's, it's . . . Zippy! No, wait, I mean Zipporah!

A: Okay, how about . . . how is God like a dental hygienist?

T: A dental hygienist? Amadeus, what on earth are you talking about?

A: I thought you knew everything about the Bible.

T: Yeah, but a dental hygienist? You're just making that up.

A: No, no, it's right there in Scripture. Look up Amos 4:6.

T: (*Hurriedly checking Bible*) "I gave you cleanness of teeth in all your cities, says the Lord."

A: See? Right there in Scripture.

T: Amadeus, you aren't taking this seriously.

A: I'm a fool—what can I say?

T: Okay, okay, but Amadeus, what does the Bible mean to *you*?

A: Well, more than just a bunch of answers to a Trivia game anyway.

T: Well, sure. I mean Bible Drill Team was fun, but that's not what the Bible is all about.

A: So what does the Bible mean to *you*?

T: Now wait, I asked you first.

A: Who's on first.

T: Amadeus!

A: Okay, okay. Let's see. Well, the Bible is the book of the church.

T: Well, sure, but what does that mean?

A: It's our foundational book, the one we all agree on . . . . (*Hears what he's saying and winces; T gives him an over-the-spectacles type of stern look*)

T: The one we all agree on? Amadeus, haven't you been reading the church papers?

A: Okay, the one we all fight over. But at least we agree that it's the one we fight over, even if we don't agree on how to interpret it.

T: I guess that means it's foundational, all right. But, Amadeus, I feel like I'm getting the official party line here. You know: "The Bible is the book of the church," "Scripture is the authoritative source and standard for preaching and teaching about faith and life," and so on, and so on, and so on.

A: Sounds right to me. Do you have a problem with that?

T: Well, not really. It's just that . . . I'd like to know what it *really* means to you.

A: Hmmm, what it *really* means? (*Thinks*) Well, the big Story means a lot. You know—God creating the world, and covenanting with a people, and the people always falling away, and God calling them back. And then there's Jesus' life and death and resurrection, and the healing that that brings the whole world.

T: Yeah, that really *is* Good News, isn't it?

A: But, Theophilus, I have to confess . . . there's a lot about the Bible that just doesn't make much sense to me. I mean, all that walking on water and feeding people in the desert and angels appearing—it's not the ordinary everyday world *I* know.

T: I know what you mean.

A: But then there are other passages that I keep coming back to, like the Sermon on the Mount, or some of the Psalms, or that Romans 8 passage about God's love . . . let's see, "for I am sure . . ." (*Breaks off, unsure*).

T: You mean Romans 8:38–39? "For I am convinced that neither death, nor life, nor angels, nor rulers, nor things present, nor things to come, nor powers, nor height, nor depth, nor anything else in all creation, will be able to separate us from the love of God in Christ Jesus our Lord."

A: That's it! I wish I had more passages memorized the way you do.

T: Well, Bible Drill Team wasn't all trivia. We did get a lot of passages down by heart.

A: So, Theophilus, what *does* the Bible mean to you?

T: Well, Amadeus, sometimes I get so mad at how the Bible gets used that I just want to throw the whole thing out.

A: Really?

T: Do you know what all the Bible has been used to support? Everything from war to anti-Semitism to the whole patriarchal system and the status quo generally.

A: And people can sound so self-righteous as they spout whatever verse supports their viewpoint.

T: Yeah, when it should be obvious to them that *my* verse and *my* interpretation is the right one!

A: Uh, Theophilus . . .

T: No, I know. I just get tired of all the wrangling that goes on.

A: I know. Sometimes I wonder if we aren't missing the whole point (*Both sigh, look discouraged, etc.*).

Older person from congregation: (*Standing*) I wonder if I might make a suggestion?

A & T: (*Looking up hopefully*) Yes?

OP: Maybe it would help if you went back to what you were originally going to talk about (*A & T look confused*). You know, the Word.

T: But that is what we *have* been talking about.

OP: Yes, but you've been focusing on the written Word. I wonder if that isn't why you are starting to feel like you've lost the main point.

A: I'm confused.

OP: (*Patiently*) The *written* Word is meant to guide us to the *living* Word of God. Knowing the biblical Story is good, knowing passages by heart gives food that sustains us, and wrestling with the implications of the Word for our daily lives is vital. But without an encounter with the living Word, we're just noisy gongs and clanging cymbals. We need to let the living Word shape us and transform us.

T: So how do we do that?

OP: Spend time with Scripture. Take the time to drink deeply and be nourished. Pray with a passage, asking the Holy Spirit to illuminate it for you, and reading it slowly, again and again. Explore it in new ways, through movement, art, drama, song. Test your insights with other believers. Live obediently. Let yourself be shaped by the Word (*Sits down again*).

A: I think maybe I'm catching a glimpse of what you mean.

T: I can think of times when Scripture has shaped me in some important ways (*Nodding agreement*).

A: And it brings a whole new dimension to who's on first.

T: Excuse me?

A: "Who's on first? The living Word." See? "Who's on first in our hearts? The living Word." Get it? (*T shakes head*) Never mind. Let's go meditate on the living Word.

CHAPTER 7

The Living Word

THE BIBLE

The Bible is the book of the people of God. It is our book, the written Word that shapes our identity as a people, gives guidance for faithful living, and provides hope and encouragement. It tells our story as a people, recording encounters with God, times we have turned away from God, and the way God keeps calling us back. It is the source for many rich metaphors and powerful images. We turn to Scripture for wisdom, for direction, for deeper understanding of and encounter with God.

We also fight over it. The Reformers declared the primacy of Scripture, and then faced an explosion of differing interpretations of Scripture. Letters to the editors of church papers draw on Scripture for their differing views on the hot topic of the day, and accusations fly back and forth that the other side is willfully ignoring Scripture, or misusing it, or, at the very least, interpreting it wrongly. History shows us that Scripture can indeed be misused and abused. Scriptural arguments have been given to justify crusades, pogroms, slavery, and other forms of injustice and oppression.

Despite the difficulties, the Bible is the book of the church. For Christians, Scripture is an essential part of congregational discernment. Conversely, congregational discernment is a vital means for our interpretation of Scripture. In the face-to-face interactions of congregational life, we wrestle with the implications of Scripture for our faith and life.

Scripture has a multi-faceted role in congregational discernment. Dwelling in the Story is basic formation work, laying the groundwork for all of our Christian life together and shaping us as the people of God. Encountering the living Word through the written word opens us to transformation, breathing the life of the Spirit into our dry bones. Wise reading in our congregational discernment leads us to faithful embodiment of Scripture in our own time and place.

DWELLING IN THE STORY

One of my pastors tells the story of a time when she was helping with the children's program at a retreat for missionaries. The group was moving from one activity to another, and this involved a long walk across the campground. Lois used the time as an opportunity to get better acquainted with Daniel, a pre-school child from a Jewish Christian family. She strolled beside him, asking the usual sorts of questions about him and his family—"How old are you? How many brothers and sisters do you have?" He chatted happily with her. Then she asked, "Now, where is your family from?" He looked up at her and said earnestly, "We were slaves in Egypt." Lois' mind whirled with the little she knew about the family. As far as she knew, they had never been in Egypt. Was there some exotic story in their background that she hadn't heard before? How could they have been slaves? Then it clicked into place. Daniel was talking about his family in the broadest sense. He identified with his people, with the Jews who were slaves in Egypt so many centuries ago. His sense of who he was and who his people were had been shaped by the biblical story so vividly that Lois was caught by a moment of wonder.

Story shapes us as a people. It gives us a common ground, a common language, a common vision. It helps form our identity, our sense of who we are, and who we may yet become. The Bible brings us the church's Story. It is literally *story*, with a large portion of it coming in narrative form. It is also the Story that shapes our identity as the people of God. As modern-day followers of Christ, we stand in a long stream of interactions between God and God's people. One way we are formed as God's children is by learning the Story in which we stand, and claiming it as *our* story, whether we come to it as blood descendants of those early Jews or as "grafted-on" Gentiles. For this Story to become ours, we need to dwell in it. We need to take the time to read it, to meditate upon it, and to hear it in worship. We listen to all the ambiguity and multiple meanings that story inherently carries. We learn it by heart, not in the sense of memorizing trivia, but by allowing our hearts and our imaginations to be shaped by this Story.

Pause for reflection

♦ *How do you feel about the Bible? Do you claim its Story as your own?*

♦ *What is your congregation's attitude toward the Bible?*

ENCOUNTERING THE LIVING WORD

Dwelling in the Story is a lifetime undertaking, but it will only be a joyful one if we move beyond a dutiful reading or a thirst for information to an encounter with the living Word.

Some time ago I interviewed one of the older members of my congregation, asking about the role the Bible had played in her life. Christine was raised in a family that valued the Bible, reading it in family devotions each day. She learned much from a beloved Sunday school teacher and from other Bible study. While she was in a lonely overseas mission setting, she was sustained by reading the Bible in depth, and down through the years she conscientiously read in it each day. This discipline laid an important foundation for her. Yet she says that it was only in her sixties, when she became a member of a small group at Church of the Saviour in Washington, D.C., that reading her Bible became a joyous task.

For this small group, reading the Bible was a vital part of their spiritual journey together. Each member would work with the week's lectionary passages throughout the week, reading them, pondering them, and reflecting on the intersection of those passages with their everyday lives. When they came together for their small group meeting, their engagement with the passages became the basis for their discussion together. They allowed the passages to speak to them and their lives, forming and transforming their actions and interactions. They encountered the living Word in their work with the written word.

It is the living Word, rather than the marks on the page, that is our primary interest, after all. The written word serves to teach us about God, but is not itself divine. The early Reformers and Anabaptists used a flock of word pictures to communicate this awareness of the relationship between Christ and Scripture. They saw Christ as the light in the lantern of Scripture, as the jewel in the casket, the sword in the sheath, the baby in its swaddling clothes, the wine in the wine-shop rather than the sign at the door. We turn to Scripture as a way of encountering the living Christ and being formed more fully into Christ-likeness.

Reading in this way does not come to us automatically. Through school and work, most of us have been conditioned to read for information. The text is "out there," material to be mastered and controlled. We come to it with our own agenda in mind, covering a lot of ground quickly, looking for answers to the questions we bring. We approach it with analytical and critical skills, assessing the material and sorting out the information we need. In its proper place, this is an important way to work with Scripture. All of us do it at times; those with special training for it can be a gift to the church.

But if this is the only approach we bring to reading Scripture, something is missing. Reading for spiritual formation calls on the use of different reading techniques and a different way of engaging Scripture. Reading for formation is slow—the goal is not to cover masses of material but to allow ourselves to find the deep wellsprings. We make space for the text to speak to us and shape us. We come to it with an openness to receive and respond, readying ourselves for transformation. The text serves as a window through which the Spirit can blow, gentle as a breeze, or strong as a gale.

Spiritual formation is not a choice; character development is not optional. We are always being formed spiritually; we are always developing some kind of character. "The question is not *whether* to undertake spiritual formation; the question is *what kind* of spiritual formation are we engaged in. Are we being increasingly conformed to the world, or are we being increasingly conformed to the image of Christ?"[1] We can choose to turn to Scripture, letting it shape our characters into Christ-likeness, and forming us as the people of God.

This does not mean that every time we read Scripture we come away with a deep sense of encounter and transformation. That's not the way it works. Sometimes transformation builds slowly. What seems to be a dry spell may be a time of laying groundwork, or of tearing down barriers we have built up. Sometimes we need to hear a message again and again until it sinks in. Insight may suddenly coalesce into a moment of revelation and change. Head knowledge becomes heart knowledge and shows in our lives.

This encounter with Scripture comes in many forms—through our private reading and prayer times, and through interactions like Christine experienced in her small group or the group *lectio divina* described in chapter 3. It can happen in Sunday worship, when the Scripture is read with care, or combined with movement that enhances meaning, or sung, or embodied in dramatic form. It can also happen in the midst of discernment. One Board of Elders chooses a Scripture passage that is their theme for the year. They read it at the beginning and end of each meeting, and at any time during the meeting any elder can "call for the Gospel." If such a call comes, the group stops what it is doing and hears the passage read again, allowing the elders to refocus and remember what they want to be about. Other suggestions for interweaving Scripture and discernment in congregational meetings can be found in Appendix A.

Pause for reflection

❧ *When has reading Scripture been joyful for you? When has it been life-shaping or life-changing?*

❧ *How does your congregation engage with Scripture?*

FAITHFUL EMBODIMENT

True encounter with the living Word is not just a matter of intellectual discussion or private devotion. It is not complete until the Word is faithfully embodied in our lives, individually and corporately. When we approach Scripture with humbleness and openness, striving to know and to do what God desires, we ask, "What difference does this make in our own lives, in who we are, and what we do? What is God calling this gathering of believers to be and to do, in this time and place?" We seek authentic continuity with the faith and witness of those first believers, who sought to live out the teachings of Jesus through the grace of the Holy Spirit.

Faithful embodiment of our encounter and relationship with the living Word means active engagement in continual change. Authentic continuity does not come from simply doing the same action. As the time and place changes, a given action will have different meanings. In order to "do the same thing," we in fact have to do something different. Simple living and identifying with the poor may mean traveling with no purse, no bag, and no sandals in first-century Palestine, wearing a rough brown robe tied with a rope in 13th-century Italy, wearing plain dark coats and dresses in 16th-century Switzerland, or wearing a simple white cotton sari in 20th-century India. In other times and places, the same garb is seen as quaint, "religious," or delightfully ethnic. It no longer conveys the meaning it had in its original setting.

The living Word became embodied in a particular historical and cultural context. Jesus walked among us as a Jew, born in first-century rural Galilee. So too the written Word was given form in particular historical and cultural contexts. The Bible is diverse, incorporating writings in different languages, from different cultures, and from time periods that span centuries. Its writers brought their own ways of seeing the world, and their own ways of expressing the inspiration they received from the Holy Spirit. While the good news they share with us is intended for people in all times and places, we, in turn, receive the Word in our own particular historical and cultural context. As we seek to embody that Word, living as faithful followers of Christ in all areas of our life, we must become wise readers of Scripture and of the world around us. Together we translate the good news here and now, discerning authentic continuity for this time and place.

TRANSFORMING ENCOUNTERS

Dwelling in the Story and encounters with the living Word are the fundamental and ongoing elements of becoming wise readers of Scripture. Our identity is shaped and our imagination formed through our meditation on Scripture. We take on and join in with God's vision for justice, peace, and righteousness. We are shaped and transformed by the

Holy Spirit. As we come together to discern authentic continuity and the faithful embodiment of Scripture in this time and place, we do so within this context. Our discernment is grounded in Scripture interpreted through the guidance of the Holy Spirit in the community of faith. For many of the decisions we address, this foundational awareness of Scripture applies whether or not there are particular verses pertinent to our decision.

Our response may also be transformed as we encounter the living Word in the midst of our discernment. I have seen this happen, and it was a particularly striking experience because it wasn't even an actual congregational discussion. Marlene Kropf, professor in Spiritual Formation at Associated Mennonite Biblical Seminary, introduced a seminary class to group *lectio divina* as a way of hearing the voice of Scripture in the midst of congregational discernment. She set up a role-play with the example of a church group wrestling with what songs should be sung in worship. The players included an energetic young woman who wanted more contemporary songs, an older man who was adamant about traditional hymns, and a number of other roles. The young woman and the older man in particular became deeply involved in their roles; the worship wars were waging full force in the middle of the classroom. The student who had the role of the pastor was feeling all the frustration that anyone trying to facilitate such a discussion feels.

When the energy was most intense, Marlene broke in with the group *lectio divina*. She invited them to take a few deep breaths and to focus on God and then slowly read Colossians 3:14–16:

> Above all, clothe yourselves with love, which binds everything together in perfect harmony. And let the peace of Christ rule in your hearts, to which indeed you were called in the one body. And be thankful. Let the word of Christ dwell in you richly; teach and admonish one another in all wisdom; and with gratitude in your hearts sing psalms, hymns, and spiritual songs to God.

She then read it a second time, inviting the participants in the case study to listen for a word, a phrase, or an image that caught their attention. After a moment or two of silence, she invited them to say the word or phrase aloud. She read the passage two more times, once with directions to listen for a connection to their own lives, and once with directions to listen for God's invitation to them through the passage.

She finished and the group once again began the discussion on what songs to use in worship. The tone of the discussion had undergone an amazing transformation. Instead of being strident and accusatory, the various players were truly able to listen to each other, and to begin finding some solutions together. As the class debriefed after the role-play, the two participants who had been most caught up in the argument both testified to the transforming effect the scriptural words had had on them, moving them from a place of hurt and anger with the other to a place where they again saw the other as sister or brother. The "pastor" talked of the way the knot in his stomach had slowly relaxed.

Our discussion acknowledged that use of group *lectio divina* could be manipulative; we saw a key element in the role Marlene played, coming in as a trusted person outside the argument, able to use Scripture to help the group remember who they were in Christ. Her role was similar to that of the *discernmentarian* in Worshipful-Work. (See Appendix A, Part I, D6 for more on the role of a *discernmentarian*.)

BECOMING WISE READERS

Formational and transformational interaction with Scripture is a crucial element of congregational discernment. It is not the only way we interact with Scripture in discernment, however. In some congregational discernment, we will want to examine particular biblical passages together. This calls for yet another way of being wise readers. In working with a particular passage, we try to hear it anew. This takes effort. We sometimes seem to have been inoculated by past exposure, sure that we know what is there. We need to slow down and take our time. What does *this* passage say? What does it *not* say? What do we wonder about as we read it? Information about the original language and the historical and cultural setting may help us hear the passage more fully, and should be shared in the congregational setting, but this careful listening is not just a task for biblical scholars. Each of us should be opening our ears and hearts, trying to receive the passage on its own terms.

We also try to hear how the passage fits into the broader biblical conversation. It is not one verse alone but the whole of Scripture that is given to us for instruction, for encouragement, and for building up the Body. How does this voice fit in with the other voices? In their book, *Seeing the Text*, Mary Schertz and Perry Yoder use the image of a tapestry for this broad biblical conversation. The tapestry is made up of threads of different colors and textures, coming together in a complex design. Some threads are thicker than others, carrying more weight or appearing more often. Some make up the background—hardly seen, but necessary to hold the whole together. Some threads come together in bundles, creating repeating patterns that stand out and dominate the tapestry. Others are minor, in colors that support or contrast with the dominant patterns.

When we look at the Bible, we can't assume a "flat text" with all threads or all voices equal. Trotting out our pet verse on the subject under discussion and assuming that that settles the debate is simply not an adequate way of honoring the richness and complexity of the biblical tapestry. Cutting out a thread because we don't like it or find it difficult is also not an adequate response. Instead we examine the various threads, seeing how they fit in the tapestry.

This is not a new idea. We get glimpses of Jesus working with Scripture in this way. In Matthew 12, he responds to questions about his disciples plucking heads of grain on the Sabbath first by referring to David and to the law about priests in the temple. Then he tells the Pharisees that there is a prominent pattern that they have missed. If they would stop fussing about minor threads and pay attention to the major pattern of "I desire mercy and not sacrifice," they would not condemn the guiltless. Similarly, in Matthew 19, Jesus responds to questions about divorce by seeing a thread of greater weight in God's purpose of unity in marriage as expressed in Genesis than in Moses' permission for divorce as given in Deuteronomy. So we, too, strive to see how our passage fits in the tapestry, and to hear how its voice fits in the biblical conversation.

We also pay attention to how the passage speaks in our own time and place. To do so, we must learn to read ourselves and our world, both the bad and the good. What forces and assumptions pull us in directions contrary to God's desires for the world? Conversely, where is the Spirit already at work in the world, going before us "into Galilee"? Where does our worldview limit the questions that we ask, or the answers we are willing to hear? What do we bring that helps us more fully hear and live out the passage today? Just as periodically we need to clear the cupboard where we store our images of God, we also need to take a good clear look at ourselves and at the world around us when we discern.

One part of doing so involves opening ourselves to hearing those voices that challenge our own interpretations, listening with respect to the concerns they bring. The history of the church is full of examples of biblical interpretations that were later seen to be faulty and self-serving. Becoming wise readers means we need to include opportunities to test our conclusions. Too often our interpretations justify the way we are already doing things. As a corrective, we need to allow other voices to challenge our interpretations.

Jesus Christ: The first and foremost "other voice" is the self-revelation of God embodied in Jesus Christ. Is our interpretation consistent with Christ's life, teachings, death, and resurrection? Does it move us toward justice, peace, and reconciliation with God and others? Does it embody the mind of Christ that Paul describes in Philippians 2?

Scripture: If we have not already explored how our passage fits in with the biblical conversation as a whole, we certainly should do so now. Are there voices in the Bible that challenge the interpretation we have reached? Are there other perspectives we should consider?

Christians in other places and times: We encounter a given passage within our own community, but we belong to the body of Christ that extends through time and around the world. How are others hearing this passage?

Those on the margins: We need to make a special effort to hear the voices of the poor, the outcast, and the oppressed, in order to offset the ease with which we hear the voices of power—our own or others. What do these voices tell us of injustice or brokenness to which we have been blind?

Pause for reflection

♪ *How does your congregation incorporate Scripture in its congregational discernment and decision making?*

How is it testing its interpretations with other voices?

How do we weigh the threads?

READING IN COMMUNITY

Wise reading may seem an overwhelming task. How are we to weigh all these important considerations? Who has the time for so complicated an effort? What happened to the clear sense of Scripture?

Don't despair! What may seem overwhelming for one person becomes possible as we work together. We bring different skills and resources and pool them together. Yes, it is complex, but we handle complexity quite well in many other settings—from six-year-olds who can spout dozens of details about the daily life of dinosaurs, to jocks who know all the strengths and weaknesses of every team in the league, to gardeners who know what plants do best under which conditions. We can live with complexity in our Bible reading as well. It takes time, but understanding the implication of Scripture for our lives and truly living it out has always taken time. It is a question of priorities.

The community of faith is the proper home for this multi-leveled reading for identity, encounter, and faithful embodiment. This community includes trained biblical interpreters, but the interpretation of Scripture cannot be left to the academic community or to church authorities. Discernment is an integral part of being the people of God. Individually and communally, we develop the practices that allow us to be shaped by Story, to encounter the living Word, and to faithfully embody the Word in this time and place. We read with discernment *for* discernment, asking what this reading means for our lives—our daily life as we scatter into many different places of interaction with others, and our communal life as we gather together.

Together we try to understand what faithful embodiment means for us. We gather as a community of faith, made up of individuals. Just as the Bible includes different voices, so does our community. We each come with our own perspectives and personalities, with different levels of study and training, different levels of spiritual maturity. Naturally there will be differences and disagreements as we begin talking together. Indeed, if there are *not* differences and disagreements, our alarm systems should go off. Dynamics such as manipulation and peer pressure can warp our discernment. Lack of questions and clear-eyed criticism can lead to disasters like the complacency of the German churches in the 1940s, the mass suicide of the followers of Jim Jones, the support for apartheid in South Africa, and the indifference to consumerism and greed in U.S. churches. And so we wrestle with our differences and challenge our interpretations with other voices, carrying the biblical conversation on into today.

Reading in community is an ongoing task as the setting shifts and changes around us, and as we take counsel and interact with others. It is a continuing conversation. Discernment does not end at the congregation's door. While necessary work happens in the face-to-face setting, we also give and receive counsel with other congregations and beyond. We make decisions using the best discernment we can, and we continue in conversation, evaluating the results of the decisions we have made. Becoming wise readers is a lifelong task for individuals; discerning authentic continuity and faithful embodiment is an ever-continuing task for the community of faith, gathered and scattered.

NOTE

1 M. Robert Mulholland Jr., *Shaped by the Word: the Power of Scripture in Spiritual Formation*. (Nashville: The Upper Room, 1985), 28.

Good-bye

Props: Colorful tie, large tarpaulin

T: Hi! I'm Theophilus.

A: And I'm Amadeus.

T: We're pilgrims on a journey.

A: Two fools for Christ who wander the world,

T: trying to put into words what can't be put into words,

A: trying to understand mystery and paradox and talk about them with people like you.

T: So, what's the word for today, Amadeus?

A: The word for today, Theophilus, is . . . *Good-bye.*

T: Good-bye?

A: Yeah, good-bye. You know—like in "So long, farewell, Auf Wiedersehn, good night."

T: Amadeus, this isn't the *Sound of Music*.

A: It isn't?

T: And anyway, we're not trying to trick this class/congregation and make an escape.

A: True. But it is almost time for us to leave.

T: But we just started this dialogue.

A: I mean, it's almost time for us to say good-bye. We're at the end of the book. It's time for us to move on.

T: More wandering the world, eh?

A: Yep, it's time to go find some others who want to talk about paradox and ministry.

T: Er-r-r, Amadeus, that's paradox and *mystery*.

A: Mystery . . . ministry . . . ministry . . . mystery (*With weighing in balance, this hand/the other hand motion*). I don't know, Theo. Are you sure there is a difference?

T: Maybe that's a dialogue for another time, Amadeus. Right now, the point is—our time here is coming to an end, right?

A: Right.

T: So do you think they've got discernment all figured out now, Amadeus?

A: It may be time for us to leave, Theo, but I think they are just beginning.

T: How can you say that? They've just spent, what, 6 or 7 weeks on this. Isn't it time for them to move on to something else as well? They ought to have discernment down pat.

A: So, how about you, Theo? We've been here all this time. Have you got discernment all figured out?

T: Well, let's see. What did we figure out?

A: (*Makes 1-2-3 conducting motion while saying*) Dis-cern-ment.

T: Oh, yeah—discernment is like listening for God's song.

A: (*Singing up the scale and back down*) Tra-la-la-la-la-la-la.

T: And joining in. But Amadeus, you're still no Julie Andrews.

A: But I can still try to come up with a gift for God.

T: Well, if it's going to be a gift of your singing, it's a good thing the Holy Spirit is around to transform us.

A: Why? Is the Holy Spirit going to transform you into an appreciative audience?

T: We're getting sidetracked here. Where were we in our learning about discernment?

A: Let's see. Discernment is kind of like singing in tune with God, and it's kind of like knowing God well enough that you can pick out a necktie that God will really like (*admiring own vibrant tie*).

T: You mean, it's like finding the right gift for God.

A: Yeah, something that fits in with what God really wants.

T: What God delights in.

A: And what God wants for the world. Remember all the emphasis on God's will being about relationship and reconciliation?

T: Yeah, it's like God is getting ready for a big party.

A: And we're all invited.

T: Along with all sorts of other strange and interesting people.

A: Whom are you calling strange?

T: We're getting sidetracked again. Let's get back to discernment.

A: Yeah, what about some of that nitty-gritty practical stuff?

T: You mean like the tools in our kit sack?

A: Yeah, and those five phases that were like kids building a marble roller.

T: (*Numbering on fingers*) Let's see: Preparing, Gathering Information, Discussion, Decision, and Implementing the Decision. And then there were those ideas for becoming wise readers of Scripture.

A: (*Numbering on fingers*) Dwelling in the Story, Encountering the living Word, Faithful Embodiment.

T: We did go over some good basics about discernment. Why do I have this feeling that discernment is maybe a little more complicated when we actually try to do it?

A: Oh, you mean complicated as in "Real life is always messier than the tidy descriptions?"

T: Mmmm . . . yeah. We've been talking the simple version here.

A: (*Nodding*) And sometimes life is like that. And sometimes it's more complicated. But do you have a better idea of the basics by now, Theo?

T: Well, I sure don't have it all figured out. But I think I understand discernment a lot better. I can see it takes some ongoing work. Some practice.

A: (*Nodding*) And some spring-cleaning.

T: Yeah. That's why I brought this tarp. (*Starts unfolding, shaking out large tarp*).

A: What does a tarp have to do with spring-cleaning? What's that for? (*T begins to drape it over A and himself.*) Theophilus, what do you think you're doing?

T: (*Stops*) Well, Amadeus, I didn't know the word for today was good-bye. I thought it would be "under construction" or something like that.

A: Under construction?

T: Well, yeah. I can see it will take some work to get this discernment stuff up and running.

A: So what's the tarp for?

T: I thought we could get under this tarp and do some discerning about our next step and where we should be heading.

A: So is this tarp big enough for this whole class/congregation?

T: Are they coming with us?

A: Not that I know of. But it is time for them to figure out what they are hearing and what their next steps should be.

T: Time to do some discerning about what God is calling them to be and do in this time and place, eh?

A: Yes, time to put on their fools' caps and risk asking foolish questions.

T: I wonder what they have been discovering about themselves and about discernment.

A: I wonder what they have been learning about the strengths they already have and what new ideas they would like to try.

T: I wonder what problems and paradoxes they will run into.

A: I wonder what mysteries and ministries they will find.

T: I wonder when we're going to be through with this dialogue.

A: And I wonder how we will ever get this tarp folded up again.

T: Come on, Amadeus. Time to go. Good-bye and blessings to all of you.

A: Thanks for having us. And "So long, farewell, Auf Wiedersehn, goodnight!"

CHAPTER 8

Discerning Next Steps

In the late 1700s, all Yearly Meetings in the U.S. agreed that owning slaves was not compatible with being a member of the Society of Friends. A long journey brought these regional gatherings of Quakers to this discernment. In 1688, a group in Germantown, Pennsylvania, brought the first written protest against slavery to their Yearly Meeting. It took eight years before that Meeting was able to agree that Friends should not encourage the importation of more slaves. While many Quakers protested slavery, others owned slaves or profited from slave labor.

It seems obvious now, but it took step by slow step, as first one Yearly Meeting and then another moved toward repudiating slavery. First there were rulings against individuals purchasing imported slaves. Then committees were set up to meet one-on-one with Quaker slave-owners to persuade them to free their slaves. By the mid-1700s, all Yearly Meetings were encouraging manumissions with compensation for past services. Finally, by the 1780s, all Yearly Meetings were taking steps to remove from their rolls any Quakers who persisted in owning slaves.[1]

In one sense, this story goes beyond the focus of this book, which is congregational discernment. Nonetheless, it is an important example. Yearly Meetings are made up of smaller Monthly Meetings—the congregational level. For all Yearly Meetings to come to a common mind, it took the culmination of discernment by many different groups, each traveling their own discernment journeys. It was an incredibly slow, painful process, especially for those who watched it as slaves. And yet, despite all the hesitations and self-serving doubts, the Society of Friends throughout the U.S. did come to the recognition that owning slaves was inconsistent with their faith. And although it took them nearly a century to do so, they still got there a century before the rest of the United States.

Discernment can break new ground, leading groups of people to creative actions. But the path of discernment is not always clear or smooth. If we come to it expecting it to be simple and easy, we will quickly get discouraged and disillusioned. A book like this can be misleading. I have been simplifying and giving the broad brushstrokes in order to build up some basic understandings. Reality is messier. Even when we come to discernment with the best of intentions, we haul along our biases, self-interest, anxieties, doubts, and fears. We fuss, and argue with one another, and generally get confused. Sometimes discernment seems to take forever.

Yet discernment does happen, despite it all. Being too pessimistic about the possibility for congregational discernment is as problematic as being too optimistic. An overdose of cynicism can short-circuit the possibilities, cutting off discernment before we have had a chance to get started. Our best approach to discernment is to come with an awareness of the difficulties, being realistic about the complications we may encounter, yet also hopeful about God's ability to work with and through our imperfections and incompleteness. We take the risk of going ahead, one step at a time, discerning as faithfully as we can, stepping forward in faith.

Pause for reflection

⚜ *Is your attitude toward discernment primarily pessimistic or primarily optimistic? What about your congregation's attitude?*

⚜ *What particular factors influence this (e.g., personality or congregational culture, particular past experiences, stories you have heard from others)?*

⚜ *What could encourage you and your congregation to take a realistic and hopeful approach to discernment?*

COMPLICATIONS

Trying to discern together can get messy. We run into complications and confusion, and we discover barriers within ourselves that keep us from being fully open to God. Despite all our efforts, we run into problems. We are uncomfortable when we disagree with each other. We try to say something and find that others have misunderstood, or heard it in a way we didn't intend. We have different styles of communication and different styles for addressing conflict. We have different frameworks for how we see the world. We have different levels of tolerance for ambiguity and different levels of patience with drawn out decision making.

Group dynamics can be a challenge. Under stress, we revert to ineffective patterns and defensive barricades. We get anxious and unwilling to move from our position. The majority can put pressure on the minority, or the minority can tyrannize over the majority. Power issues can flare up, with each of us sure that someone else has more power than we do. We get stuck in our differences.

Fortunately, while complications do arise, for the most part we are able to handle them. We get things sorted out, find resolutions, and move on. When we do encounter cases that are more complicated and unyielding, we need to turn to additional resources. Written resources and workshops on conflict transformation and mediation can be helpful. We should not hesitate to call for help. The perspective of someone who is not in the middle of the confusion and the conflict can often help us see what is happening. Trained mediators or facilitators can guide us through the rough spots. Many denominations have suggestions for people that can be drawn on for this sort of assistance.

BARRIERS

As we work with discernment, we find ourselves encountering barriers within ourselves and within the community that can make discernment more difficult. Sometimes the barrier is something simple that can be easily fixed—for example, recognizing that it is difficult to talk to each other when we meet in a worship space with fixed pews facing the front. The congregation can then address this barrier by choosing to meet in another, more flexible setting, where participants can see each other's faces.

Other barriers are more complex. Sometimes we will be able to do something to remove them, and other times we will only be able to acknowledge that they are present. What follows is not intended as an exhaustive list, but as a way of raising awareness of potential barriers. Being aware of them and talking about them together can help us to find ways of working with the realities of our personal and congregational situation.

Individual barriers
- Personal style: "I can't stand a lot of meetings and talk"; or "I like the give and take of debate!" or "Can't we just get to the point and decide?"
- Mental or physical health: "My energy is absorbed by a health issue and I have none to spare for congregational discernment at this point."
- Habit: "But I am used to *this* way of doing things."
- Self-doubt: "I have trouble speaking up in a group. I feel I can't speak articulately or think clearly enough. Why should my voice matter?"
- Negative past experiences: "I was betrayed by a group that got into a real snarl trying to reach consensus."
- Skepticism: "How can we really know what God desires?"
- Fear: "What if God wants us to go in a direction I don't want to go, or that demands too much of me?"
- Lack of self-awareness: "I have no problems—of course I know God's will."
- Self-deception: "My reasons are all good, upright, and just."
- Inappropriate expectations: "You haven't really heard me or you would agree with me."
- Assumptions about others: "Someone who disagrees with me is just too fearful, or too obsessed, or too radical, or too hidebound, or too . . ."

Congregational barriers
- Lack of meaningful relationships and trust
- Ingrained habits: the need to "be nice"; non-participation; debate mode; passive-aggressive behaviors; unhealthy uses of power

- Knee-jerk mistrust of leadership as being manipulative and controlling
- Untrustworthy leaders who *are* being manipulative and controlling
- Expectation of uniformity; discomfort with difference and ambiguity
- A culture that values competition, efficiency, and productivity more than relationships
- Prosperity and possessions, security, and certainty
- The time and effort required for discernment
- Uncertainty: "How do we do this?"
- Space or setting that is not conducive to conversation and reflection

Pause for reflection

♯ *What barriers do you recognize in yourself?*

♯ *What barriers do you see in your congregation?*

♯ *How might you begin addressing such barriers?*

GOD'S PROJECT

As we reflect on how to increase the discernment in our congregational decision making, it is good to remember where this goal originates. God desires for us to be a discerning people. Helping us to become a more discerning people is God's project, not ours alone. This awareness shapes our approach to the project. We can treat the question of how to increase our discernment as itself a question for discernment. We can be attentive to the steps the Holy Spirit is nudging us to take.

A woman involved in decision making at the regional and denominational level has a personal story of such a nudge. Jane was participating in a several-day meeting of regional representatives. The structure this group used was to work in tables of eight, staying with the same group for the entire time. The evening before the session began, Jane arrived at the conference center and checked the list of working groups.

She discovered that George, a representative from another region, was to be part of her group.

From things she had heard from others, Jane knew that George's views on the issues they would be discussing were quite different from her own. She was anxious about how they would work together. In the middle of the night, she woke up with a clear sense of God saying to her, "You need to ask George how he came to his position."

Jane has learned to be attentive to such nudges so, even though she couldn't see what difference it could possibly make, the following morning she approached George and, rather sheepishly, explained that during the night she had heard that she needed to ask him about his story. They sat and talked over breakfast. As Jane listened to him, she learned that his position had shifted. She was also able to identify several values they shared. These discoveries released Jane from her fears and freed them both to work constructively together through the rest of the gathering. Even more, it provided the basis for a new friendship.

God is at work in many different ways, drawing us towards reconciliation and deepening our discernment. We may be nudged to a small personal action, as Jane was. Listening and responding to such nudges helps us develop our discernment skills further. We can also seek to discern together what steps God may be inviting our congregation to take. Each congregation has its own unique set of group dynamics and past experiences. What is fitting as a next step in one congregation will be different from the next step for the congregation down the road. Each congregation can listen attentively to discern the steps that will move it toward deeper discernment.

CONGREGATIONAL STORIES

While we need to discern the appropriate next steps for our own congregation, hearing what others have done can suggest new possibilities. In the winter of 2003, I interviewed pastors from a dozen Mennonite congregations that are doing discernment in one way or another. These congregations are scattered across North America. They include large and small congregations, rural and urban, long-established and newer churches. Some have well-developed structures for discernment and decision making; other pastors were quick to say that their congregations were just taking baby steps in incorporating discernment into their decision making. None of them feel that they have it all figured out. They recognize that working at discernment is an ongoing process. There is always something to be learned and to be done differently next time. I share some of their stories not to suggest that they have found the one right way to do things, but to show some of the varied ways congregations are incorporating discernment. Their stories can encourage our conversation as we seek to make discernment a more vital part of our own congregational practices.

Waterloo North Mennonite Church is a young, urban, highly educated congregation of about 250, located in Waterloo, Ontario. A conference-facilitated church plant, it began about 17 years ago and quickly grew. Like many other urban congregations started in the past few decades, in the early days it was very deliberate about its decision making, expecting high participation at its monthly meetings. It used a mixture of consensus and voting, with invitations for all to respond in writing to express their degree of agreement with a consensus statement.

Two intense discernment processes in its early years—one on a controversial issue that involved 14 meetings in a 24-month period and the other on a building project—left the congregation's members burnt out with such highly participatory decision making. And as their numbers grew larger, old patterns didn't fit any longer. For a period of time, they were content with one annual business meeting.

In more recent years, the leadership has been attempting more deliberately to include discernment in the congregation's decision making. One step has been to end each church council or ministry team meeting with the question, "Where are we seeing God at work in our midst?" Pastor Sue Steiner says that this initially was a stretch for some. "A few didn't say anything for three or four meetings," she says. "But then they started joining in and it has become an important reflection time for us."

For several years, the ministry team has set a theme verse for their annual general meeting. Throughout the meeting there are reflective interludes for prayer, song, and hearing the verse read. They have also begun asking three or four people to pray for congregational meetings while they are occurring, with one person asked to pray specifically for the chair of the meeting. This prayer group is usually off in the prayer room, though they may also move in and out of the meeting, or even be praying for the group from a different location.

In addition to the current pattern of biannual members' meetings, for the past several years they have been in a period of discerning future directions. This has involved additional times of gathering for discernment. There have been a series of meetings led by a congregational member who has significant experience in facilitating group discussion as a professional mediator. She has been able to lead the meetings in creative ways, so that interest in decision making has been reviving, with 100 or so of the congregation's 175 resident members coming out for the meetings.

They continue to work with the differing views in the congregation about discernment and how long it takes. "It's a delicate balance," says Steiner. "Some need to see that something is moving forward, while others are willing to take time. We keep looking for methods that allow participation and movement." There are also different views on how much decision making to delegate to the leadership groups and what kind of decisions all should participate in. They are also getting used to their size, and finding what works best with the larger group. As they write new bylaws for the congregation, they are trying to hold all this in their awareness, rather than locking themselves into something they will not want to use later.

First Mennonite Church in Beatrice, Nebraska, is a traditional rural congregation of about 180. Coming from the Prussian/Russian strand of Mennonites, it recently celebrated its 125th anniversary. It has a long history of active involvement in the broader church and in the local community. For over 50 years, the congregation regularly welcomed Associated Mennonite Biblical Seminary students as summer pastoral assistants, helping them grow into their pastoral role. In cooperation with Beatrice Mennonite Church, it built a deaconess hospital and then administered it for 65 years. More recently, the two congregations started the first daycare in town and initiated a Mother to Mother program. Eventually these programs grew too big for the congregation and were handed over to the larger Beatrice community.

First Mennonite also has well-established ways of making decisions. In former days, the annual business meeting was a major event. It included meals and thorough discussion, and lasted two full days. Now there is an annual business meeting and another semi-annual meeting, each an evening meeting. Projects and facility decisions are made and the nominating committee's slate of congregational appointments is discussed and voted on.

While the traditional ways of making decisions continue, the congregation is expanding the ways it works with discernment and decision making. Several years ago the Deacon Board undertook the work of creating a new vision statement. Initial work done at an evening congregational meeting was developed and revised by the pastoral team and the Deacon Board, before being adopted by the congregation. Now this vision statement is shaping the congregation in a number of ways. It is part of the liturgy used in Board and Church Council meetings, a liturgy that begins with lighting a candle and opening themselves to God's presence, and then proceeds with repeating together their purpose statement, working through their agenda and offering prayers of gratitude, and closing with a benediction.

The statement also provides the basis for continuing vision work. Since 1980, the congregation has been divided into eight to twelve Shepherd Groups, each with a "shepherd." These groups include all in the congregation, even those who are non-resident, and are reorganized every second year. They are the place for welcoming, inclusion, and practical care, and meet in homes on a monthly basis. For the past two years, the congregation has asked these groups to use their January meetings as a time to discern and develop details of the basic vision statement.

The agenda for this small-group discernment time is thoughtfully prepared. Once a year the pastors and deacons take a weekend retreat and concentrate on one element of the vision statement. This past year, for example, they focused on the third line of the vision statement, "God calls us to . . . Carry the Good News." Together they spent time in Bible study and reflection, discerning how that one concept could be fleshed out in the congregation. The questions, ideas, and proposals that came out of this retreat time then were passed on to the Shepherds by the pastors. This provided the agenda for further congregational discernment in the Shepherd Groups. While a number of ideas were discussed, the sub-point that caught the imagination of the Shepherd Groups was, "By imitating Christ in our neighborhoods and workplaces." This led to a Sunday morning series called "Work as Mission." Members shared about their work, the pastors preached on work, and the series culminated with an invitation for everyone to create their personal mission statement and bring it as a gift. Co-pastors Weldon and Florence Schloneger hope that such work will eventually culminate in new vision for congregational mission.

Akron Mennonite Church is a 45-year-old suburban congregation with 450 members, located near Ephrata, Pennsylvania. Their small fellowship groups used to be the primary way of processing congregational decisions, but the congregation moved away from this as small groups wanted to spend less time on congregational business and more time on personal sharing. In 1997 they were operating with an annual business-meeting model, when they invited Marlene Kropf from the Mennonite Board of Congregational Ministries to guide them in a weekend workshop on discernment. That workshop led them to move to a quarterly discernment model.

For their quarterly discernment Sundays, instead of having Sunday school, they gather around tables in groups of eight to make decisions about budget, bless the annual slate of committee selections, consider proposals from the leadership group, and work with other congregational decisions. The time begins with a meditation to set the tone of the meeting, and they have used silence, or prayer, or song before decisions as a way of allowing space for the Spirit.

Recently they entered a time of more intense discernment, a time of focusing on vision work and exploring new directions for the congregation. Initial work was done at a missional vision retreat; then four focus groups each developed further ideas that were generated at that retreat. The whole congregation was invited to be part of the discernment for one Sunday school quarter. For those thirteen weeks, they followed their usual quarterly discernment pattern and gathered in groups of eight around tables each educational hour. Each table had a facilitator, who received some orientation and then regular coaching by e-mail from the steering committee. The focus groups brought specific proposals to these sessions, which were then discussed by the table groups. All comments were recorded and available later for Sunday school teachers and others who couldn't be present.

They also tried something new for them, the use of two "discern-mentarians." This is a concept that comes from the Worshipful-Work model. Two people from the congregation were invited to fill the role of offering observations on the process or suggestions for prayer and song that could keep the group attentive to God's presence. Co-pastor Jim Amstutz provided some training for them, drawing on denominational writings by Marlene Kropf and the book, *Discerning God's Will Together*, by Morris and Olsen.

"The process itself has changed us," say Amstutz and co-pastor Dawn Yoder Harms. "How we are getting there is part of what we are doing differently." Eighty or 90 people were involved in the table discussions each week, and 150 turned out for the last Sunday and the vote on new directions. Amstutz and Harms are enthusiastic about the formation of ministry teams, and the new directions the congregation is moving with missional work and with discernment.

Jubilee Mennonite Church is a small congregation of 60 or 70 where the number of people under age 13 equals those over 13. Twenty-five years old, it is located in downtown Meridian, a small Mississippi city. They have two congregational meetings in August, and another in June. They try for consensus, but they also vote. "If we only make decisions through consensus, all power goes to the persistent dissenter," says co-pastor Elaine Maust. "We take enough time to test whether the dissent is a prophetic word, but we're also ready to go on and move to a vote even if not all have agreed."

The pastoral team considers it an important priority to cultivate a congregational culture of discernment. This begins with the pastors and other leaders taking the time to seek counsel, pray, and listen to God. It also involves encouraging their members to listen to the many different ways God speaks, and to name the ways they see the Holy Spirit breaking out. One way that Maust approaches this is in the context of the worship committee, encouraging them to talk about what is happening in worship and to name where they see the Spirit at work.

Prayer plays a vital role for their discernment. "We want to create an atmosphere where saying 'I want to pray about this' is not a cliché," Maust says. "We come with a sincere question. We don't know yet what we'll do about whatever it is: small groups, a Bible school coordinator, continuing our tutoring program. We come with the expectation that something will come out of the prayer. It anticipates God's action." She goes on to acknowledge that the congregation struggles with prayer. "There have been times when desperate, earnest prayer didn't come out the way we wanted, but we have also seen miracles."

Prayer permeates congregational life, through Sunday pastoral prayers, prayer in congregational meetings, and prayer groups. For some big decisions, like whether to purchase the huge old Presbyterian building they now meet in, the congregation has held 24-hour prayer vigils. The congregation also names intercessors as part of their annual gifts discernment. In recent years, this group has been anywhere from three to six in size, and has included a 40-year-old wise "elder," a ten-year-old girl with a gift for prayer, an oil rig drilling supervisor who prays at work, and a non-English speaking older woman, among others. Anyone in the congregation can ask one of these intercessors to pray for them; the elders also contact them about congregational decisions that need prayer.

Such a focus on prayer and discernment has guided the congregation as it has made decisions about mission. "We have endless possibilities here in Meridian, but as a small, mostly working- and middle-class congregation, we don't have endless resources." They bless and encourage those who want to be involved and contributing elsewhere, but as a congregation they have been called to two primary congregational ministries: a tutoring ministry with a $200,000 endowment and a near-by church camp. These are major commitments for a church their size.

Pause for reflection

❧ *What steps do you see these congregations taking? Would any be fitting for your own congregation?*

❧ *Are you aware of other congregation's stories and practices that might suggest possible next steps for your own congregation?*

DEEPENING OUR DISCERNMENT

Each congregation will need to find the steps that work for it in deepening its discernment, but there are some areas we can all consider. The best place any of us can start is by developing our own personal practices of prayer and attentive listening to God. This is important for pastors and other congregational leaders, but also applies to the rest of us. Prayerful listening and testing, paying attention to the biblical conversation, and reflecting on our lives from a faith perspective will help us all to grow as discerning Christians.

Some congregations will need to learn more about discernment. Books like this one, sermons and discussion times, workshops, and retreats can help to raise new options and provide the chance to try new tools. With interest and awareness, the congregation may want to try some baby steps. Instead of dashing into the marathon of the most controversial issue facing the congregation, begin with smaller congregational settings. Elder or deacon groups can be a good place to develop discernment skills. Some leadership groups and committees have found the book, *Transforming Church Boards into Communities of Spiritual Leaders*, by Charles Olsen, to be a good resource for this.

Other congregations are deepening their discernment by training people to serve as support groups for discernment with individuals. Two books by Suzanne Farnham and others, *Listening Hearts: Discerning Call in Community* and *Grounded in God: Listening Hearts Discernment for Group Deliberations*, are designed to help with such an approach. Skills in discernment learned in these smaller settings begin to spread out and influence other congregational settings.

Many congregations have found that discernment related to future directions captures the imagination and interest of their members. This seems to be an area where we more easily see the possibility of discernment in action. *Discerning Your Congregation's Future* by Roy Oswald and Robert Friedrich Jr., and *Discerning God's Will Together* by Danny E. Morris and Charles Olsen, are two resource books that focus on this sort of vision work.

Don't overlook some of the background work that provides a foundation for our congregational discernment. The Philippians' prayer we looked at in chapter two suggests that our love for one another is what makes discernment possible. We may need to explore ways of increasing our fellowship and building loving relationships. If trust has been shattered, we have catch-up work to do before we can attempt to discern together. Cultivating our ability as individuals and as a congregation to see clearly and to speak the truth in love is also important, as Paul wrote to the Galatians and the Ephesians. We may need to spend time becoming wise readers of Scripture. Learning to recognize and name the work of the Spirit in our midst is another important step. Worshipping and praising God is ongoing work of the church that also helps us grow as a loving, thanks-giving, discerning people. Strengthening such foundations will also strengthen our discernment.

Pause for reflection

❧ *What foundations do you need to strengthen? What foundations does your congregation need to spend time strengthening?*

❧ *What is the one "next step" that you or your congregation could take to deepen their discernment?*

NOTE
[1] Margaret Hope Bacon, "The Abolition of Slavery," in *The Quiet Rebels: The Story of the Quakers in America* (New York; London: Basic Books, 1969), 94–121; and Thomas E. Drake, *Quakers and Slavery in America* (New Haven: Yale University Press, 1950).

A Fools' Kit

PRACTICAL SUGGESTIONS FOR DISCERNMENT PROCESSES

This appendix provides suggestions and practices that can be help-ful in congregational discernment. Think of it as similar to the large, loose sack the Fools carry. They collect odds and ends along the way, and bring them out later, when they need them in a dialogue. The sug-gestions in this appendix are drawn from mediation and conflict trans-formation work, from spiritual direction practices, and from the discernment practices of other Christian groups like the Quakers and the Jesuits. Your congregation may want to adopt some of these as reg-ular practices; others will be brought out only occasionally; some may not fit at all. This kit sack can be a beginning point for congregational discussions about what practices could help your congregation. As you talk together, you may discover other good practices that individuals in your congregation have picked up on their own journeys that can be shared and added to your congregational repertoire.

This appendix includes references to a variety of books and resources. The complete publication information for each appears in the Bibliography.

A Fools' Kit Outline

Part I—Before the Meeting(s)
A. Physical Preparations
B. Mental Preparations
C. Spiritual Preparations
D. Planning the Meeting (s)

Figures
1. Assumptions for Congregational Work
2. Discernment Listening Guidelines
3. Hand Mnemonic as Listening Guideline

Part II—Suggestions for Facilitators

Part III—Group Activities That Cultivate Discernment
A. Five Minutes of Silence
B. Telling Our Faith Stories
C. Writing Psalms of Lament
D. Weaving Biblical Story with Congregational Story
E. Scripture Meditation
F. Group *Lectio Divina*
G. Examine the Cons and Pros
H. Seeing the Good and Strengthening Options
I. Testing an Option

Part IV—Reaching a Decision
A. Testing for Agreement
B. Spectrum of Dissent
C. Gradations in Voting
D. Saying "Yes!"

PART I. Before the Meeting(s)

A. Physical Preparations
1. Choose your meeting location with care. Gathering in your worship space may be an aid to integrating worship and decision making, if the seating arrangement does not limit interaction. Gathering in your fellowship hall may be a good reminder of community, if noise and visual distractions can be kept to a minimum. Be creative in adapting your setting to aid your discernment.
2. Aid face-to-face interaction. Arrange chairs in a circle or semicircle(s). Larger groups can gather in small groupings, e.g., around tables of eight. Make sure that all can hear—use a portable microphone if necessary.
3. A visual focus can remind us of God's presence in our midst. Consider having a central table with a candle or symbols significant to the congregation, a special banner, or a "set aside" empty chair.

B. Mental Preparations
1. Make it easy for people to attend. Choose a meeting time that is convenient for as many as possible. Provide childcare so parents can be present. Consider holding your meeting for discernment before or after a potluck meal, or in connection with a gathering for worship.
2. Provide information in appropriate form and length beforehand. Printed information may be needed for complex topics; a simple verbal announcement may be fine in other situations. Some congregations make a practice of presenting the query and background information, and having initial discussion at one meeting, and then waiting until a later meeting to finish their discussion and come to a decision.
3. Agree on general guidelines for discernment meetings, and review these together periodically. Consider making the guidelines available for participants to reflect on prior to meetings, or go over a few at the beginning of each meeting. Figures 1–3 (p. 171-173) offer several different approaches to such guidelines. For complex decisions that will involve numerous meetings, you may want to create a covenant, with agreements specific to that process.

C. Spiritual Preparations
   1. Encourage all participants to be holding the meeting and the facil-
      itator(s) in prayer beforehand. For major decisions, consider set-
      ting aside a specific time(s) or location where participants can
      gather to pray and reflect prior to meeting for decision. There is
      a long Christian tradition of fasting in connection with prayer
      and discernment—some may want to commit to fasting and pray-
      ing one day a week in preparation for a challenging discernment,
      or one meal a day in the week leading up to a challenging meet-
      ing.
   2. Encourage prayers with an inward focus: asking God for insight
      into the decision, for awareness of my own blind spots, and for
      willingness to release my fears.
   3. Encourage prayers with an outward focus: asking God to
      strengthen the bonds of love in the congregation, to give us the
      grace and curiosity to hear each other, and to bring clarity to our
      discernment.
D. Planning the Meeting(s)
   1. Plan the agenda with care. Limit the number of issues addressed
      so you have adequate time for discernment. Ask: "How can we
      help prepare a way for God's presence to be felt in our work?"
      Incorporate practices that will help you move beyond the usual
      verbal and rational processing.
   2. Plan for trust-building and relationship-building. How will you
      care for one another during this discernment? Take into consid-
      eration the ways your congregational discussion may affect indi-
      viduals, and plan ways to support those who are vulnerable. On
      many issues this will not be a major factor; on others it will be
      crucial. Provide support groups or one-on-one pastoral care as
      needed.
   3. Consider having the congregation form a prayer together. Olsen
      describes a church board that uses the saying, "We are forming
      our prayer." Drawing on Matthew 18:19 ("If two of you agree on
      earth about anything you ask, it will be done for you by my Father
      in heaven"), they feel an important prelude to any decision is to
      agree on what their common prayer will be. If you are working
      with a troublesome issue, what laments, confessions, and peti-

tions concerning it do you wish to bring before God? If you are working with vision and planning, what are you asking God to help you do together?

4. Plan to incorporate prayer throughout your meeting. Name congregational intercessors, either as an ongoing ministry team, or for specific meetings. These intercessors can hold the meeting in prayer in the midst of the gathering, or in a nearby room, or even from another location.

   In *Transforming Church Boards*, Olsen suggests rotating prayer during Board meetings, assigning each elder a 15-minute block during the meeting in which they are to pray silently for each person in the group and for the discussion in which they are involved. This could be adapted for use in congregational meetings by inviting people to sign up for a certain time period during the meeting. Olsen has a number of other suggestions for making prayer an integral part of Board meetings that might also be adapted for congregations.

5. Choose a theme verse for a particular meeting, or as a congregational focus for a year. The Lord's Prayer, the Beatitudes, and many of the prayers in the epistles can serve well in reminding us of whose people we are and what we are to be about. The facilitator can call for a few minutes reflection on the verse as a way of re-focusing a discussion that has gotten overly heated or off track.

6. Choose facilitators with care. Avoid conflict of interest issues— if a proposal is being brought to the congregation, have someone other than those bringing the proposal facilitate the discussion. In *Discerning God's Will Together*, Morris and Olsen suggest that just as groups using Robert's Rules of Order may have a parliamentarian, so groups doing discernment may want to name a *discernmentarian*—someone who is paying attention to the spiritual dimensions of the meeting. She or he may guide the group's deliberations, or may be a resource person, working in conjunction with another. Consider naming co-facilitators, dividing the role to have one who is focusing on moderating the meeting and another who is focusing on the spiritual dimensions.

7. Plan how you will keep participants informed. The time of the meeting, the agenda, and any information to be read ahead of

time should be available at least a week before the meeting. With decisions that involve a series of meetings, consider having tapes or minutes of the meeting available for those who miss a particular session. In a given meeting, briefly review the earlier work that has been done.

FIGURE 1

Assumptions for Congregational Work

1. We are open to hearing God's call.

2. Everyone has wisdom.

3. We need everyone's wisdom for the wisest result.

4. The wisdom of the whole group is greater than the sum of the parts of the group.

5. Everyone gets to hear and be heard.

6. What each person brings to the process is recognized as authentic.

From Jeff Steckley, Giving Project Consultant Coordinator, Mennonite Church Eastern Canada—adapted from "Clashing Images of Participation" by Jo Nelson and Brian Stanfield, in the August 2000 issue of *Edges*.

FIGURE 2

Discernment Listening Guidelines

1. Take time to become settled in God's presence.

2. Listen to others with your entire self (senses, feelings, intuitions, imagination, and rational facilities).

3. Do not interrupt.

4. Pause between speakers to absorb what has been said.

5. Do not formulate what you want to say while someone else is speaking.

6. Speak for yourself only, expressing your own thoughts and feelings, referring to your own experiences. Avoid being hypothetical. Steer away from broad generalizations.

7. Do not challenge what others say.

8. Listen to the group as a whole—to those who have not spoken aloud as well as to those who have.

9. Generally, leave space for anyone who may want to speak a first time before speaking a second time yourself.

10. Hold your desires and opinions—even your convictions—lightly.

From Suzanne G. Farnham, et al., *Grounded in God*, copyright ©1999 by the Christian Vocation Project/ Listening Hearts Ministries. Used by permission.

FIGURE 3

Hand Mnemonic as Listening Guideline

Thumb: Listen with your mouth shut.

Index finger: Listen with your eyes on the speaker.

Middle finger: Listen rather than thinking about your next point.

Ring finger: Listen with your heart: Exercise compassion.

Pinky finger: Listen with your head: How does what is being said make sense?

Thanks to Rachel Miller Jacobs, pastor at Kern Road Mennonite Church, South Bend, Indiana, who learned this from Kathy Shreiner, a fifth-grade school teacher in Mishawaka, Indiana, who uses it in her classroom.

PART II. Suggestions for Facilitators

The following list is intended as a set of suggestions, not specific steps that must be followed. The items are numbered for ease of reference.

1. Review the overall agenda for the meeting at the beginning of the meeting.

2. Have someone introduce the issue to be discussed, providing a brief background and enough information to help people get on board.

3. Be aware of different learning and communicating styles. Some people need to hear information; some need to see a written handout or notes on newsprint; some need to be moving and actively engaging with the information in some way.

4. Be clear about what the group is being asked to do: share information, air concerns or define a problem, generate possible solutions to a problem, weigh several proposed options, modify a specific proposal, respond yes/no to a specific proposal, dream about the future, and so forth.

5. Use a portable microphone as a way of slowing the pace of the discussion and of making it clear who has the floor, in addition to helping with hearing.

6. Help the group to stay focused. Intervene to bring conversation back to the topic; recognize when a tangent is fruitful and name what is happening; bring in reminders of God's presence as needed; clarify what the group is being asked to do if there is confusion.

7. Pay attention to who isn't speaking as well as to those who are. If a few voices are dominating, ask those speakers to allow others to speak before they have another turn.

8. Help keep the meeting a safe place for everyone. Intervene in cases of overgeneralization, blaming, speaking for others, interrupting, withdrawing, or personal attacks. (See Schrock-Shenk, *Mediation and Facilitation Training Manual*, page 222 for some ways to respond to such situations.)

9. Clarify and summarize comments when necessary, or have speakers summarize. Avoid unnecessary filler—some comments need no clarification or summary.

10. Give the group permission for reflective silence by stating your own comfort with it. Learn to distinguish fruitful silence from lack of communication.

11. Use individual reflection, one-on-one time, and discussion in small groups as ways of bringing in the voices of those who are uncomfortable speaking in a large group.
12. Have someone record ideas and questions on newsprint so they don't get lost.
13. Use a newsprint record as a quick way to review work done at a previous session. Post the newsprint and invite people to take a "gallery walk" in groups of 2–4, reminding themselves and each other of what has been done earlier. Such a gallery walk can also be a way for work done in small groups to be shared with the larger group.
14. Use sticky dots as a way of prioritizing options or questions that have been generated during a brainstorming session. After recording the brainstorming ideas on newsprint and posting this on a wall, give each participant three dots to put beside the options they favor or the questions they consider most urgent.
15. Use a Five Finger Straw Poll[1] to uncover questions and reservations that have not yet been spoken, or to get a quick read of where the group is. The facilitator clearly restates the proposal and reminds the group of the scale:

5 Fingers = I can fully support the proposal as it stands.
4 Fingers = I have a few reservations, but am generally supportive.
3 Fingers = I am neutral; the proposal is just okay.
2 Fingers = I have serious questions or reservations about this proposal, but would not block the group if it wants to move ahead with it.
1 Finger = I have major problems with this proposal and would choose to block the group's action.

Each person then responds to the question by holding up the number of fingers that indicate their level of support for the proposal. The facilitator follows up by inviting those who have indicated one or two fingers to express their concerns. Those showing threes might be invited to suggest improvements to the proposal. If some have chosen not to indicate any level, the facilitator may inquire about their response to the proposal. If only fours and fives are showing, the group can move on to conclude their discussion and make their decision.

16. Allow for the option of postponing a decision when disagreement is strong or there are questions to be resolved. If postponing a decision, be clear on what the next steps are and who is responsible for them. Know when a decision *must* be made.

17. Don't hesitate to call in help for challenging decisions. People with training in mediation and conflict transformation work can be a wonderful resource. They bring experience with systems theory and group dynamics that may be important for understanding what is happening in your congregation. They also bring experience with tools which may be helpful to your situation, but which are best done either by, or under the mentorship of, someone with training and experience in using them.

PART III. Group Activities That Cultivate Discernment

A. Five Minutes of Silence

Quakers call for periods of silence and attentive listening to the Spirit when the verbal discussion becomes unproductive. Olsen says, "After twenty minutes of debate and discussion over an issue on which people seem divided, the egos take over."[2] Learn to be silent together, focusing your attention on God. Many of us in North America are not used to corporate silence; the facilitator can relieve anxiety by letting the group know he or she will close the silence after a specified time. You may need to begin with silence of only a minute or two, gradually extending this as you become accustomed to it. Olsen suggests the following questions for those who need some focus for their silence:

1. Am I closing myself off from information that we need to make this decision?
2. Whom do I need to forgive to be more fully present here?
3. What is an image of God that needs to come to bear in this setting?
4. How does the Scripture that we read shed light on us now?
5. Am I operating in a need-to-win or need-to-save-face mode?

B. Telling Our Faith Stories

An important step in discernment can be the telling of faith stories—the ways we sense God is at work in our lives in relation to the topic being discussed. Olsen uses this approach extensively in *Transforming Church Boards*. The group can be invited to share such stories from their own lives or from the life of the congregation. This may happen informally in the midst of the discussion, or may come more formally, with notice of a session for such story telling being announced ahead of time or with specific people being asked to tell their stories. It may also be important to hear stories from Christians in other times and places, or from our church history. The stories chosen should be integral to the discernment, and, as one pastor from South Africa warns, should include stories from the edge as well as from the center. Together we listen for the ways God is at work, building up the body, revealing areas of blindness, and producing fruits of the Spirit.

For more about telling faith stories, Luke Timothy Johnson's *Scripture and Discernment* is an extended exploration of the role of such story telling in Acts and its implications for today.

C. Writing Psalms of Lament[3]

In some discernment situations, it will be appropriate to write psalms of lament. Over half the psalms are of this type—the psalmist expresses trust in God, laments a particular situation, and calls on God to act, promising to praise God when God has acted. A lament is not whining; it is calling out to God, naming the pain or fear or anger we carry, and petitioning God to do something about it, all within a framework of trust in God's care and ability to act. We can write our own laments, or write a lament on behalf of another. The latter calls for careful listening to truly understand the other's lament.

As part of congregational discernment, individuals could be invited to write their own psalms of lament, or challenged to write a lament on behalf of someone with whom they disagree. Or the congregation may choose to write a lament together, calling out to God about a pain or an injustice they hope to address through their discernment.

D. Weaving Biblical Story with Congregational Story

One way to allow Scripture to speak to a particular decision is to let the biblical story interact with our congregational or personal stories. Steps one and five can be done in the congregational setting; the rest should be done in smaller discussion groups. Olsen models this type of story weaving throughout his *Transforming Church Boards*, and describes several variations in chapter four. He provides cautions and encouragement—the goal of story-weaving is to make a space for Scripture to speak in our conversation, not to end discussion. We should not be intimidated by the idea of biblical-theological reflection, nor feel it is only the role of the pastor. It is something we can do together, as a congregation, and it is an integral part of discernment.

1. Tell a congregational or personal story. Choose one that is significant for the decision. There may be a congregational story that should be retold and remembered. Or the congregation might invite individuals to share a personal story of the way the issue has touched their lives.

2. Select a Scripture passage. In silence, ask the Holy Spirit for a passage that will illuminate the discussion. A story, person, theme, verse, or image may come to mind. Participants share these nudges and the group chooses one to focus on.

3. Read the passage out loud. What happens in the text? Who are the players, their roles and feelings? What is the face of God in this text? How is God at work? What invitations are there for the people of God?

4. Weave the stories together. Reflect theologically on the two stories. Does the biblical story bless and affirm the congregational story, or does it contradict and confront it? Does the biblical story nudge us in a new direction? Does it transform the congregational story into something new? What do you discover as you look at them side by side?

5. Identify insights gained from this story-weaving and explore how they apply to the congregational discernment.

E. Scripture Meditation

Another way to allow Scripture to have a voice in discernment is to include a time of Scripture meditation. This can be a guided meditation around a passage chosen by the facilitator or the planning group, or a more open time of meditation, with several options available for responding to a passage.

With a guided meditation, the facilitator can lead the group into being present with a particular biblical story, walking them through the events and allowing space for each one to connect with it in a personal way. Or the biblical story may be the entry into a more general meditation time. *Opening to God*, by Carolyn Stahl Bohler, is one resource for such guided imagery meditation on Scripture.

Another option is to provide a passage for meditation, or to generate one as a group, and then to have available different ways of working with the passage—perhaps room for a prayer walk, or praying with clay, or providing paper for drawing or writing. The Listening Hearts Discernment group provides suggestions for such responses in its *Retreat Designs and Meditation Exercises*.

F. Group *Lectio Divina*

Lectio Divina is yet another way to allow Scripture to speak to our discernment. A partial description of one time of group *lectio divina* can be found in chapter 3. There it was a regular practice of a weekly fellowship group. Norvene Vest describes this spiritual practice in *Gathered in the Word: Praying the Scripture in Small Groups*. In a slightly modified form, group *lectio divina* can also serve to re-center a discussion and to allow the living Word to speak to us through the written Word in the midst of discernment.[4]

Before the meeting, the facilitator or *discernmentarian* chooses a number of passages that may be appropriate. Ideally they will be fairly short, be pertinent in some way to the topic, and serve to open us to God's presence. If it seems appropriate to use one of these passages, invite the group to:

1. Take a few deep breaths, in order to become present to the moment and to God.
2. Listen for a word, phrase, or image that attracts their attention, as the passage is read out loud two times. In the minute of silence after the passage is read, they should stay with that word or image,

murmuring it over and over, savoring it. The leader then invites people to call out the word or image that has come to them, without elaboration.

3. Hear the passage read a third time, with the invitation to listen for how this passage touches their life today. A memory or image or a sensory impression may come to them during the two minutes of silence after it is read. The leader can invite a few people to share briefly what came to them, or simply allow the group to do silent reflection.

4. Hear the passage read a fourth time, listening for a possible invitation relevant to the discernment the group is engaged in. After a few moments of silence, the leader invites those who wish to share their invitations with the group to do so.

5. The leader closes the *lectio divina* with prayer, thanking God for the ways the Spirit has moved through the written Word.

G. Examine the Cons and Pros

This method allows the group to work together, first in all being *against* the proposal, then in all being *for* the proposal. It is done within a context of prayerful preparation for "holy indifference" to anything except the will of God.

1. Present the proposal to be considered, with time for questions of clarification.

2. Allow time for prayerful consideration of the proposal.

3. As a group, focus on the cons. List all the reservations and reasons to not go with the proposal. Include both head and heart reasons. In smaller settings, each person can be asked to give their responses. Something unexpected may come out at this point which makes it clear the discussion should go no further, otherwise the group continues with the remaining steps.

4. Allow space for prayerful consideration, perhaps even scheduling separate meetings for considering the cons and pros.

5. As a group, now focus on the pros. List all the reasons for going with the proposal.

6. Weigh what has been said, determining which alternative seems most reasonable to the group.

This approach to weighing of pros and cons comes from the Ignatian tradition. Joan Mueller's *Faithful Listening* and Pierre Wolff's *Discernment* describe this approach in much fuller detail than is possible here.

H. Seeing the Good and Strengthening Options[5]
In decisions where the congregation is looking at several options, consider a step of seeing the good in each option. Most of us tend to see the problems first. It can be a good exercise to begin by naming the good before moving into discussion.

1. Introduce the options, providing necessary information and clarifications.
2. Address one option at a time, asking the group to name the good they see there. Record these strengths on newsprint and post in a visible location. Consider the future as well as the present: what opportunities are here? No weaknesses are pointed out and there is no debate over the relative merits of the options.
3. After all the options have been addressed, take a brief time for reflection and prayerful consideration of the good that has been recorded.
4. Again speaking to one option at a time, improve the options. What would make this option stronger? Record these improvements on the newsprint.
5. The facilitator restates the new, improved options. It may already be apparent that one option is the strongest. Or several may have been combined into one option that all can support. The congregation moves on to weigh the options and to reach their decision.

I. Testing an Option
When the group is moving toward one or two choices, but before the final decision is made, the group can take a step of testing an option. Even if the group has settled on one option, it is appropriate to take a time-out to test what spirit the group senses, before moving ahead with a decision. Those in the Ignatian tradition talk about listening for consolations and desolations. At a simple level, this involves sitting with one particular option and listening with one's heart. Does this option move toward life and love, or away from it? Does it bring a sense of peace,

or of dis-ease? Does it draw the group closer to God and God's desires for the world, or does it move away? What would be the ramifications if the group goes ahead with this decision? What sort of fruits might this option produce?

The Ignatian work with consolations and desolations is more fine-tuned than we can go into here. Joan Mueller's *Faithful Listening* and Pierre Wolff's *Discernment* are two resources for exploring this approach further.

PART IV. REACHING A DECISION

A. Testing for Agreement

When the discussion appears to be drawing toward a conclusion, the facilitator tests this with the group. He or she should not take silence for consent. Formally, the facilitator can propose a minute, a restating of the conclusion the group seems to be reaching. This minute may undergo further conversation and modification before agreement is reached. Informally, the facilitator can test for agreement with statements such as, "I hear us saying . . . . Is this what you all are hearing?" or "My sense is that we have agreement on . . ." In each case the facilitator should state as clearly as possible the conclusion he or she is hearing, but present it tentatively, allowing room for corrections and disagreement.

Throughout the conversation, participants should be aware of their responsibility to speak up in a timely fashion with any reservations or objections. We want to avoid a false consensus that lasts no further than the door of the meeting room. As a conclusion nears, the facilitator should take special care to see that any remaining reservations, questions, and objections are brought up. He or she may ask for such reservations ("Are there any objections to the proposal that . . . ?") or may try stating the possible agreement in the negative ("Is there anyone who does not agree that . . . ?"). Another way to bring such reservations and questions into the open is to use the Five Finger Straw Poll described above, under Suggestions for Facilitators. Note that it is a tool for reaching consensus, not a vote. Even when no questions arise as a result of the show of hands, the facilitator should go on to name the consensus that has been found and ask for a nodding of heads or other sign of agreement, rather than assuming it on the basis of the Straw Poll.

B. Spectrum of Dissent

Quakers traditionally work with a pure consensus model. If one member can't agree with the direction the group is going, in theory the whole group is blocked from proceeding. The reality is more nuanced. Quakers have a spectrum of dissent available to them, ways they can express disagreement while permitting the group to go ahead. Other groups can adapt this spectrum to their own setting. Some points on the Quaker spectrum:

"I disagree, but do not wish to stand in the way." There has been sufficient interaction, with time for response to people's questions and discussion of reservations and disagreement. The group appears to be moving toward a particular consensus, but some are still uncomfortable with the decision. They can choose to withdraw their opposition without withdrawing their disagreement. In essence, they are saying to the group, "I am not convinced that this is the best decision, but I don't feel so strongly about it that I must block it. I am willing for the group to go ahead."

"Please minute me as opposed." Similar to the point above, speakers taking this approach are continuing to disagree, but are not blocking the group's decision. They are asking to have their opposition recorded in the minutes, but not choosing to stop the decision. If many people ask to be recorded as opposed, the group likely has not done adequate work with its effort to reach consensus and should not assume it has reached a conclusion.

"I am unable to unite with the proposal." Even this statement, which has the effect of blocking the group from moving ahead with its decision, may not be the final word. It does mean no decision will be made at that meeting. But before the next meeting, work will be done to see if there are questions or reservations that can be cleared up, or if personal interactions with the individual may bring a change of heart. Having expressed strong opposition, the speaker may become ready to move to one of the other points on the spectrum, still disagreeing, but not blocking. At other times, of course, the individual remains unable to agree with the proposal and the group will not proceed.

A longer discussion of these levels, including evaluations of many aspects of the Quaker way of making decisions, can be found in *Beyond Majority Rule* by Michael Sheeran.

C. Gradations in Voting

There are also variations possible with voting. We often think of voting as yes/no, either spoken, or by a show of hands, or by ballot. One way of bringing gradation into voting is by allowing different percentages for different decisions.

Some decisions may appropriately be made by a simple majority vote; others, such as the calling of a pastor, are better set at a higher percentage, such as 80 per cent. Another gradation can be brought in with the use of a written ballot that presents options other than a simple yes/no, or that provides space for written comments explaining votes against the proposal. Decisions about percentages needed, how abstaining ballots are treated, and who is eligible to vote should be made before the discernment conversation begins.

D. Saying "Yes!"

Many congregational decisions are satisfactorily noted by the facilitator announcing the results of the vote, or by the facilitator stating the consensus to which the group has agreed.

Some decisions are best met with a moment of silence and respect for those who have disagreed. At other times, however, we want to celebrate the hard work and good conclusion that we have come to together. Some decisions call for special ways of saying "yes and amen" together. We want to laud the unanimous vote, or go beyond simple head-nodding when the facilitator asks if we have come to consensus. The facilitator might invite a spoken amen, call for song, have all who support the decision stand, or invite the group into a prayer of praise and thanksgiving. Explore these and other ways of saying, "It has seemed good to the Holy Spirit and to us."

NOTES

[1] Thanks to Carolyn Schrock-Shenk for this modification of the Straw Poll found in Mennonite Conciliation Services' *Mediation and Facilitation Training Manual,* 232; originally published in *Conciliation Quarterly*, Vol. 12, No. 4 by Susan H. Shearhouse. Copyright © 1993, Mennonite Conciliation Service.

2 Olsen, *Transforming Church Boards*, p. 22.

3 Thanks to Ron Guengerich whose Associated Mennonite Biblical Seminary class on the Psalms introduced me to the importance of writing laments.

4 Thanks to Marlene Kropf, associate professor in Spiritual Formation and Worship at Associated Mennonite Biblical Seminary, for this variation of group *lectio divina*.

5 This approach combines and adapts suggestions from Olsen, *Transforming Church Boards*, 96; and Morris & Olsen, *Discerning God's Will Together*, 83.

Leader's Guide for *In Tune with God* Group Study

INTRODUCTION

This appendix has suggestions for group sessions to accompany each chapter. These sessions are intended to initiate discussion and to provide opportunities to try out some of the practices described in the book. Leaders should adapt the session to fit the size and time limits of their own group. More is included than can be fit into the normal Sunday school time. You may want to consider spending two Sundays per chapter—one more head-oriented, with a focus on discussion, and the other more heart-oriented, with a focus on trying out one of the suggested practices. Or you may choose to hold group sessions in an evening meeting, when more time is available. Do experiment with some of the different modes (discussion, journaling, meditations, role-plays). An approach that is a stretch for one person may be exactly what another needs. Discernment is strengthened when we learn a variety of ways of working together. Leaders are encouraged to read over the Suggestions for Facilitators in Appendix A and incorporate these where possible.

Help your group to make the transition from busy lives, or the bustle of a fellowship break, by beginning with an opening ritual. Your work with discernment is a form of prayer. You could begin with the lighting of a candle, the repeated singing of a simple song, or several minutes of focused silence. If your group is not accustomed to public silence, this could be a good opportunity to develop the skill. See Five Minutes of Silence (Appendix A, Part III, A) for suggestions on how to go about this. Another possibility for an opening could be to read a theme verse together, aloud, such as the Lord's Prayer or Ephesians 3:14–21. The weekly repetition of such a prayer can help remind us of why we are working with this material.

Each session includes some suggestions for theme-related songs from *Hymnal: A Worship Book* (HWB), the Mennonite and Brethren hymnal available from Brethren Press and Mennonite Publishing Network. These can be used to open or close your time together. You may want to use the same song as an opening each week. Good songs for this could be:

- Hear thou our prayer, Lord (*HWB* 23);
- O Christe Domine Jesu (*HWB* 113);
- Gentle Shepherd, come and lead us (*HWB* 352);
- Lord, listen to your children (*HWB* 353);
- They that wait upon the Lord (*HWB* 584); or
- Gathering Chant (see below, page 188).

Chapters two through eight each have an accompanying "Dialogue for Two Fools for Christ." These can be presented after the opening as a way of reviewing the chapter before launching into a discussion or activity, or, in some cases, at the end of the session as a way to wrap things up. Cast and any props needed are given at the beginning of the Dialogue. They take about eight to ten minutes and will go better if the readers have a chance to run through the Dialogue together before doing it for the group.

Suggestions for the sessions include discussion questions and ideas for exercises or practices related to the chapter's material. When a reference is given to Appendix A, look there for a fuller description of that practice. If you are experimenting with a practice that is new to your group, take a few minutes to debrief and discuss how it went after you have finished it. It can be revealing to hear how differently people experience the same event. You may also want to reflect on whether it is something that might be incorporated into your own congregational discernment and decision making.

Gathering Chant

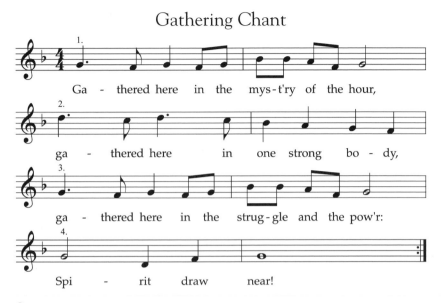

Ga - thered here   in   the   mys-t'ry   of   the hour,

ga - thered here   in   one   strong   bo - dy,

ga - thered here   in   the   strug-gle   and   the pow'r:

Spi - rit   draw   near!

Canonic voices may enter every measure.

Text and music: Phil Porter. Copyright © 1990 Phil Porter, 669A 24th St., Oakland, CA 94612. Used by permission.

SESSION 1

Prior to the session, read chapter 1 of *In Tune with God: Singing God's Song.*

Opening

Song Suggestion: Gentle Shepherd, come and lead us (*HWB* 352)

Discussion and Practices

♪ Discussion

If the group has formed specifically to work with the topic of discernment, invite participants to share briefly why they are interested in this topic.

♪ Telling Our Faith Stories (Appendix A, Part III, B)

Ask people to share stories from their past experiences of congregational discernment and decision making. How do they sense

God has been at work in their lives in relation to congregational discernment? Provide an opportunity for each person to speak. If group size makes it difficult to do this together, consider breaking into smaller groups for this sharing.

ʂ Reflection

Hand out paper and pencils. Invite the group to find comfortable but alert sitting positions. Encourage them to take several deep breaths, becoming aware of God's presence with the group. Remind them of Jesus' promise, that where two or three gather in his name, he will be there among them.

After a few minutes of centering silence, slowly read the following passage from chapter 1:

> Picture [discernment] as music and movement . . . . Picture God, singing us a song—a free-flowing song of creation and of steadfast love, of righteousness and peace. God yearns for the whole universe to join in singing this song, adding complex harmonies and improvising a joyous dance. When we discern, we listen attentively in order to sort out what is God singing and what is mere static and noise. We let the song sing through us and shape us, so that we can join in harmoniously, responding to God's love and mercy. We watch for Jesus, the Lord of the Dance, so we can join him. And sometimes, as we watch and listen and join in, we sense a nod from the Divine Singer, inviting us to pick up on a particular phrase of the music and to play with it in our own unique way, moving and singing.

Invite the group to respond to this metaphor through silent reflection, writing or drawing. After adequate time for individual work, open a time for those who chose to do so to respond in the large group setting.

Closing

This is an especially appropriate session to end with song. Seek ye first the kingdom of God (*HWB* 324) and Thuma mina (*HWB* 434) are two possibilities.

SESSION 2

Prior to the session, read chapter 2 of *In Tune with God*: Determine What is Best. Encourage participants to bring their Bibles to the session.

Opening

Song suggestions: Hear thou our prayer, Lord (*HWB* 23) Lord, listen to your children (*HWB* 353)

Dialogue for Two Fools for Christ: Discernment

Discussion and Practices

⸙ Reflection

What comes to mind when you hear the words "congregational discernment"? How does your congregation use the phrase?

Reflect on this individually, journaling if you wish. Share your reflections in pairs. In the full group, have someone record on newsprint as people call out briefly what comes to mind for them. You may want to take time for explanations if the brief version is obscure.

⸙ Group Discussion

- How do you respond to an understanding of congregational discernment as a corporate spiritual discipline?

- What attitudes toward discernment and decision making are prevalent in your congregation?

- What methods of decision making does your congregation use? What have you experienced in other congregations?

- In what ways is your decision making a "creative, informed, attentive, and interactive practice of the church, led by the Holy Spirit"?

⸙ Encountering Scripture

As a group, or in smaller groups of three or four, review the three biblical voices covered in the chapter.

a. Descriptive stories from Acts

What happened in each story? What decision did they face? Who made it? How? What elements of worship and what methods of decision making were used?

b. Prescriptive passage from 1 Corinthians 14
   What does Paul have to say about gathering for worship? What elements of worship does he mention? What does Paul have to say about discernment?

c. Prayer from Philippians 1
   What elements of discernment does Paul mention in his prayer? What does Paul see as the purpose for the Philippians' discernment?

d. After reviewing the passages, reflect on the following questions together. You can look for the common threads in all the passages, or choose one passage to focus on.
   • What face of God do you see in these passages?
   • What face of the people of God do you see?
   • What connections do you see to your own life and experience?
   • What invitations do you hear?

⟡ Forming Our Prayer (Appendix A, Part I, D3)

a. Invite participants to journal individually on the following questions:
   • What are your hopes for this study?
   • What desires do you have for your congregation's discernment and decision making?
   • What requests concerning its discernment do you want to bring before God?

b. In the large group, invite people to call out phrases that could be in the prayer. Have someone record these on newsprint and post it on a wall.

c. Give each participant three sticky dots (available in office and school supply stores). Ask them to put one dot beside each of the three phrases that most reflect the prayer in their own hearts.

d. With this information visible to the group, decide together on what prayer you will pray together. Record the prayer on newsprint and post.

e. To close your time together, pray the prayer out loud together. You may want to include this prayer as a regular part of opening or closing your sessions.

SESSION 3

Prior to the session, read chapter 3 in *In Tune with God*: Worship God Truly.

Opening

Song suggestions: Lord Jesus Christ, be present now (*HWB* 22); O worship the Lord (*HWB* 124); and Praise God, the Source of life (*HWB* 95)

Discussion and Practices

✤ Reflection

Spend time individually jotting down your own images of God. Put a star by those that have been especially life-giving. Put an X mark by those that are negative. Share your reflections in pairs. Return to the full group for a general sharing time.

✤ Group Discussion

a. Love-spilling-over: God's unchanging will

• How does your congregation nurture relationships among congregational members? How do you encourage deepening relationships with God?

• What relationship-building elements do you, or could you, include in your congregational discernment?

b. Power with vulnerability: God's interactive will

• What are some ways you have experienced power used to dominate, manipulate, or control?

• Where have you seen power used positively, empowering others?

• What empowering elements do you, or could you, include in your congregational discernment?

c. Empowering presence: God's invitational will

• What is your congregation's attitude toward the Holy Spirit?

• In what ways do you, or could you, open yourself and your congregation to the Spirit's guidance in discernment?

✤ Group *Lectio Divina* (Appendix A, Part III, F)

Prior to the session, choose one of the following passages for this exercise: Isaiah 49:15–16a, Psalm 36:7–9, or Luke 15:21–24. Explain to the group that you will read the passage aloud several times, followed by a brief silence. Each time there will be an invitation to what they are to listen for in the reading and to reflect on in the silence. You will end the silence with a question and the group will respond one at a time around the circle. They always have the option of saying "Pass" instead of responding.

a. Invite the group to set aside any books or papers and to sit comfortably alert. They should close their eyes and take a few deep breaths, becoming quiet and fully present.

b. Invite them to listen for a word, phrase, or image that attracts their attention as the passage is read aloud two times. In the minute of silence after the passage is read the second time, they should stay with that word or image, murmuring it over and over, savoring it. End the silence by asking people to name the word or image that has come to them, without elaboration.

c. For the third reading, invite the group to listen for how this passage touches their lives. A memory, an image, or a sensory impression may come to them during the two minutes of silence after the passage is read. End the silence by asking people to share briefly what came to them.

d. For the fourth reading, invite them to listen for a possible invitation relevant to the next few days and then to ponder that during the several minutes of silence. End the silence by inviting each to share their sense of invitation.

e. Close the *lectio divina* with prayer, inviting each person to pray, silently or aloud, for God to help the person on their right respond to the invitation received. This can be done simultaneously, or one-by-one around the circle. If the latter, those praying silently should end their prayer with a spoken amen so that the next person knows when to begin.[1]

🍃 Writing a Psalm of Lament (Appendix A, Part III, C)

Present the information about writing psalms from the Appendix. Use Psalm 142 or Psalm 22 to illustrate the way the psalmist cries out to God with very specific laments while continuing to express trust in God's response.

Encourage participants to write their own psalm of lament or a psalm on behalf of someone else. Spend time writing individually, share in pairs, and then in the larger group. Some will just have begun to jot down ideas, while others may have a complete psalm to share with the group.

Closing: End the session with the Dialogue for Two Fools for Christ: God.

SESSION 4

Prior to the session, read chapter 4 of *In Tune with God*: Discerning God's Will.

Opening

Song suggestions: Breathe on me, breath of God (*HWB* 356); Oh, have you not heard (*HWB* 606); Grant us, Lord, the grace (*HWB* 388) (good for closing this session)

Dialogue for Two Fools for Christ: God's Will

Discussion and Practices
§ Encountering Scripture
   Discuss Romans 12:1–2 as a group or first in smaller groups of 3–4, then share particular insights in the larger group.
   • What face of God do you see in this passage?
   • What face of the people of God do you see?
   • What connections do you find to your own life and experience?
   • What invitations do you hear?
§ Group Discussion
   • Hebrews describes a sacrifice of praise that is expressed in both words and actions. In what ways do you, or your congregation, offer a sacrifice of praise? Where does it happen through words? Where through deeds?
   • Four frameworks for understanding God's will were presented in the chapter: determinism, deism, modernism, and postmodernism. What frameworks are present in your congregation? How do you hear them expressed?

• How do you understand God to be at work in the world? What ways of talking about God's will are comfortable for you? What ways are positive, but more of a stretch?

Guided Meditation on The River of the Water of Life (Ezekiel 47: 1–12 and Revelation 22: 1–2)

This is an exercise that uses God's gift of imagination to enter into a passage of Scripture. First read the two Scripture passages out loud. Then invite the participants to find a sitting position in which they can be alert and comfortable. Have them close their eyes and take a few deep breaths to relax and center themselves. Read the following meditation out loud, pausing at the ellipses:

Imagine yourself in a grassy meadow . . . Walk a little way, feeling the warmth of the sun on your shoulders . . . Become aware of a crystal-clear river in front of you, the river of the water of life . . . Wade into the water . . . Feel the water around your ankles . . . Feel the riverbed under your feet . . . When you are ready, move to where the water is deeper, deep enough that you can swim or float . . . If you are unable to swim or float, ask for assistance, and receive what comes . . . Let yourself be carried by the waters of the river . . . Become aware of the life around you . . . Notice the fruiting trees on the banks of the river . . . Notice the birds of the air above you and the colorful fish in the water below you . . . Notice if there are other people floating in the river with you . . . Acknowledge their presence in some way . . . Become aware of God's presence and love carrying you and everything in the river . . . Look around for a symbol or image of what God desires for you . . . Remember this symbol and give thanks to God for it . . . Know that you can return to this river whenever you wish . . . When you are ready, say amen inwardly and open your eyes.

Spend some time debriefing what happened for the participants during this meditation. Ask about both objective and subjective dimensions: how the meditation unfolded for them and how they felt about it.

SESSION 5

Prior to the session, read chapter 5 of *In Tune with God*: The People of God. Encourage participants to bring their Bibles.

Opening

Song suggestions: Heart with loving heart united (*HWB* 420); You are salt for the Earth (*HWB* 226)

Dialogue for Two Fools for Christ: The People of God

Discussion and Practices
§ Group Discussion
- How does your congregation welcome imperfect pilgrims?
- In what ways is your congregation uniform? In what ways is it a unified diversity?
- How does your congregation typically respond to conflict?

§ Reflection on Response to Conflict
  Do individual journaling, then share responses to the questions in pairs:
- What is your typical personal response to conflict? Do you avoid it? Provoke it? Reluctantly address it? Seek a compromise? Find creative resolutions?
- Think of some specific episodes of conflict in your congregation. What was your role? How did you respond to the conflict? How was your response like or unlike the response described in Matthew 18?

§ Encountering Scripture
  a. Invite the group to explore Matthew 18. What are the basic sections of this chapter? Record this outline on a blackboard or newsprint. What is the theme of the chapter? What title would you give it?
  b. Focus in on the parable of the unforgiving servant. Who are the players in the story? What are their roles? Actions? Feelings? What is the face of God in this passage? How is God at work? What invitations are here for the people of God? If there is time, act out the story.

c. How does this parable fit into the overall flow of chapter 18?
d. What are the implications of this passage for your congregational discernment?

§ Bible Story Weaving (Appendix A, Part III, D)
Form small groups of three or four. Tell the story of the Square Dance Controversy (see below), or choose an appropriate story from your own congregation. The story provided is based on an actual congregation's experience, though some small details have been changed or streamlined. Follow the directions in Appendix A for weaving this story with a biblical story. Come back into the large group and compare group experiences. How might it feel to use such an approach in the midst of congregational discernment?

The Square Dance Controversy

Jen is a member of the worship commission for her small rural congregation. In a congregational brainstorming session in the spring, someone had suggested that, since they no longer had regular Sunday evening services, it would be good to have some special activity once a month. Jen and several others on the commission got excited about the possibilities and planned a list of monthly events to begin the following autumn. They saw these special events as one way of reaching out to their community, and they planned to advertise them, expecting to draw in local community members as well as the congregation. The worship commission approved their plan and the proposal was reported to the Church Council, who raised no objections.

It is now the second weekend in September. Tonight is the first session of several evenings of an annual mission festival at the church and the square dance is scheduled for next Sunday evening. As part of their plans to advertise to the community, the planning committee rented a large portable sign and yesterday, Saturday, they set it up in the church parking lot. In bold bright letters, it announces to the community that there will be a square dance at the church next Sunday and that everyone is invited. Jen thinks it looks cheerful and inviting and she is enthusiastic about this new form of outreach.

After Sunday school this morning, an older member pulled

the pastor aside to report that their Sunday school class had been talking about the sign. Another stopped him in the parking lot to say, "Some of us are very angry about that sign," and then left abruptly. After dinner, yet another member of the class called, concerned about the level of upset she heard in the class. Some were bothered by the aesthetics of the sign, while others were upset that it advertised the dance rather than the mission festival. Some didn't think the church should be sponsoring a dance, and some wondered what other churches or the community would think of them. Most of them felt the sign had been sprung on them inappropriately.

The pastor consulted with the chair of the worship commission and they agreed that they would provide an opportunity for anyone who wanted to stay and talk about the sign after the worship service that evening. When the chair of the worship commission called Jen that afternoon to alert her to the meeting, Jen was quite surprised to learn there was a problem. It had never occurred to her that either the dance or the sign might upset anyone, and she knew that they had gone through the proper channels in proposing their plan. Some of the members of the Sunday school class were part of the Church Council that had heard about the plans in the spring. She wasn't sure what all the fuss was about. She wonders what will happen in the evening meeting.

SESSION 6

Prior to the session, read chapter 6 of *In Tune with God*: The Creative Play of Discernment.

Opening

Song suggestions: Gathering Chant; Jubilate Deo omnis terra (*HWB* 103)

Dialogue for Two Fools for Christ: Process (you may want to close your session with this, rather than begin with it)

Discussion and Practices

❧ Group Discussion

- What does your congregation do, or what could it do, to nurture the attitudes toward self, others, and God described in the chapter?
- What are the expectations of leadership in your congregation? How have you experienced leaders setting the tone for discernment, being a non-anxious presence, and helping the group to remember their identity as God's people?
- Turn to the Five Finger Tool (Appendix A, Part II, 15) and the Spectrum of Dissent (Appendix A, Part IV, B). Would either of these, or something similar, be useful in your congregation?

❧ Practice Five Minutes Silence (Appendix A, Part III, A)

Invite participants to focus on opening themselves to God's presence.

❧ Case Studies

The following two congregational stories can be used as case studies by pausing at the asterisks and brainstorming ideas for how the group might shape a process of discernment for the decision described. Or you can use the entire story and explore how these two actual congregational decisions compare with the outline given in the chapter. Another option is to use a recent decision made by your own congregation. The first five sections of reflection questions in chapter 6 provide specific questions for examining and evaluating the process that was used.

Story A: Running Out of Space

Holly Road Mennonite was a growing urban congregation with space needs. For five years, Holly Road had formed a Facilities Committee each fall and each year the committee brought the congregation a list of options. Many were explored: beginning a second congregation, holding two Sunday services, remodeling, renting, buying or building a larger building. The congregation had not been able to agree on any of them. The previous year's efforts ended with several highly stressful meetings and then an evenly split vote on the option of buying a nearby empty church building, a vote that fell short of the 66 per cent needed for approval.

During those five years, the congregation had continued to grow, from an average Sunday attendance of 100 to 160 or more. The congregation was at maximum capacity and pushing building code regulations in a number of areas. Several of the options that had been explored earlier would no longer meet the situation. There was a lot of energy in the congregation, thanks to the growth and a well-respected pastor, but there was also a lot of frustration and anger over the crowdedness and the group's inability to find a solution. The Leadership Team recognized that the group no longer had the luxury of being undecided. The two main choices appeared to be either remaining one congregation (which would mean renting or buying a larger building) or some variation of becoming two (two services in separate locations, two congregations in the same building with one meeting at an alternate time, two separate congregations). The Leadership Team began planning a process to decide between these choices.

***You are part of the Leadership Team for Holly Road Mennonite. Begin brainstorming ideas for what the discernment process might look like. Be creative. You may want to move to evaluation of the ideas as a second stage, but don't do so during the brainstorming.*

Continuation of Holly Road's Story

The Leadership Team created a two-stage plan. The first stage was deciding what their process should be and having the congregation agree to it; the second stage was the process itself. Between October and February, a draft of this discernment plan, with its two stages, went through repeated revisions as it was shared with other groups in the congregation (elders, Facilities Committee, Finance Committee, Church Council). The Team put much of their initial work into carefully shaping the question the congregation would be deciding, recognizing this would in turn shape the discussion. After input from the revision process, the question they finally settled on was, "Would we rather become two, or would we rather stay together as one congregation?" In February a final version of the plan came to a congregational meeting. After discussion, the congregation voted to accept it.

Stage two moved into the agreed upon decision making process. The Leadership Team prepared a hand-out with the advantages and disadvantages of each of the options, and encouraged the congregation to expand these. In March and April, the congregation spent the Christian Education hour discussing the issue of becoming two or remaining one congregation. The series had been carefully prepared and listed in the discernment plan. The sessions included an introduction to the Mennonite statement on Agreeing and Disagreeing in Love, time for looking at the pros and cons of the two options, a straw poll, the sharing of faith perspectives, work in small groups, a questionnaire, and brainstorming. The conversation was lively and opinions were still strong. The sessions were taped for Sunday school teachers and a written summary prepared each week for those who couldn't attend. Results of the questionnaire were shared at the annual meeting near the end of the series.

Drawing on the information gathered through these congregational discussions, the Leadership Team drafted a proposal, which was then sent to Church Council for their improvements and approval. The written proposal went to church mailboxes, and two weeks later, came to a congregational meeting for "discussion and improvements." A second meeting had been scheduled if needed, and was used. Finally, at a mid-June meeting, the congregation voted by 96 per cent to stay together as one congregation, well above the minimum 70 per cent affirmative vote specified in the plan. Later that summer they approved (by 89 per cent) the purchase of another church building that had become available, and in September they moved in, taking a new congregational name since they were no longer located on Holly Road. Their new space served them well and the congregation continued to grow in the years after the move. Several years later the pastor described the mood of the congregation since the move as "positive, enthusiastic, and joyful" and the process as one that had been of tremendous benefit to the congregation.

Story B: Church Building as Sanctuary

Greenville Friends Meeting was a congregation of 40 or 50, located in a mid-western university town. The Meeting included members ranging in age from childhood to 83 and from life-long Quakers to passers-through who were attracted by the group's silent worship. They had a well-established pattern of monthly meetings for business, held after meeting for worship and a potluck, as well as a monthly Forum, an evening meeting that was sometimes informational and sometimes recreational.

Jim and Tina, members of the Meeting, were also part of an ecumenical group interested in supporting the Sanctuary movement. This church-based movement had begun earlier in the 1980s in response to a growing influx of Central American refugees entering the U.S. illegally to escape persecution and civil war, particularly in Guatemala and El Salvador. Since the U.S. government was supporting the governments of these two countries, it was difficult to obtain refugee status, and the immigration authorities often deported the refugees. A Presbyterian church in Tucson, Arizona, had taken some of these undocumented immigrants into their church building, drawing on the centuries-old concept of a place of worship as also a physical place of sanctuary. This action became a movement that spread, and congregations across the U.S. were declaring themselves sanctuaries and hosting one or more refugees.

The ecumenical group wanted to find local congregations who would consider such an undertaking, despite the risks of legal actions. For planning reasons they were hoping to get relatively quick responses from the churches they approached. Tina carried the request to Ministry and Counsel, the leadership group, asking if the Meeting would be open to such a possibility.

*** *You are part of Ministry and Counsel. You have agreed that the Meeting should look at the question of whether it would be open to declaring itself a sanctuary congregation, hosting an undocumented refugee. Brainstorm plans for how you will work on this decision.*

Continuation of Greenville Friends Story

At the next monthly Meeting for Business, the clerk (facilitator) of the meeting introduced the question to those present and outlined the plan for working with the question. At that month's Forum they would host visitors from a sanctuary congregation in a nearby city. Because of the desire for a quick response, before the next monthly Meeting for Business there would be informal gatherings in homes for those who wanted more information. The question would then come to the next Meeting for discussion and discernment.

The process unfolded as planned. Representatives from the sanctuary congregation spoke about their decision and how it was playing out as they hosted a young teenager who had fled from Guatemala to avoid being drafted by either the guerrillas or the army. Alex, the refugee, had accompanied them and he also told a little of his story, with the help of a translator. Later in the month, a number of people attended the informational sessions in homes. These gatherings were small and informal. People were able to speak freely and ask questions about what was required from a hosting congregation and what the legal implications might be.

At the next Meeting for Business, the group began as usual with ten minutes or so of silent worship. Then the clerk opened the question of whether or not the Meeting should become a sanctuary congregation. The discussion was lively, also as usual, as members raised questions or affirmed parts of the proposal. Quakers have a long tradition of faith-inspired civil disobedience, but they also do not enter it lightly. A few were concerned about possible legal repercussions. Some were eager to do something for the refugees. Others questioned second-guessing the decisions of the government authorities.

It soon became clear, however, that the real hurdle came from practical considerations. The input by the sanctuary congregation had made it clear that a major commitment of time and energy and Spanish speaking was crucial. The members were not sure that they had the resources to do it, especially because most of those who were willing to put in time and energy, and who spoke Spanish, were either graduate students who were likely to leave before long, or were only marginally involved in the Meeting. If the Meeting was going to take on such a relationship, they wanted to be able to carry through with it adequately, knowing that it could be a long-term responsibility. Jim and Tina acknowledged that their interest was not enough to carry the commitment the Meeting would need to make.

As the discussion seemed to be coming to a conclusion, the clerk tested a minute. "I am hearing us say that we cannot host an undocumented refugee. But I am also hearing interest in supporting the work that the ecumenical group is doing." With a bit more conversation, the group agreed that he was reading the Meeting correctly. A member of Finance Committee suggested a sum of money that the Meeting might be able to contribute, and as others seemed agreeable to it, the clerk amended the minute to include the suggestion. The group also affirmed the work that Jim and Tina were doing with the ecumenical group.

Jim and Tina were disappointed, but felt that the Meeting had made the right decision, given the level of resources and commitment that long-term members felt able to make. The rightness of the decision was also confirmed a few months later, when Jim, one of the few Spanish speakers in the congregation, unexpectedly changed jobs and moved out of town.

SESSION 7

Prior to the session, read chapter 7 of In Tune with God: The Living Word. Encourage participants to bring their Bibles.

Opening

Song suggestion: Lamp of our feet (HWB 312)

Dialogue for Two Fools for Christ: The Word

Discussion and Practices
❧ Encountering Scripture

Return to the Group Lectio Divina in session 3 and repeat the exercise, using another of the suggested Scripture passages.

If time constraints kept you from doing the Guided Meditation on the River of the Water of Life in session 4, it would also be appropriate here. Likewise, any of the Encountering Scripture exercises (found in sessions 2, 4 and 5) could be done now if you didn't get to them earlier.
❧ Scripture Top Ten
a. Invite the participants to spend a few minutes jotting down the

ten biblical passages that capture for them the most important threads of the biblical tapestry. These should be brief passages (ten verses or less) that point to larger themes; listing "The Book of Acts" is too broad, but its theme might be seen as encapsulated in Acts 1:8 ("But you will receive power when the Holy Spirit has come upon you; and you will be my witnesses in Jerusalem, in all Judea and Samaria, and to the ends of the earth").

b. After some time for individual work, spend time sharing in the group. What are the passages that you find foundational? Are there surprises as you talk together about these?

♦ Reading Scripture Together

a. Return to one of the Scripture passages you worked with earlier in this series (Romans 12:1–2, Ezekiel 47:1–12, Matthew 18:23–35) or use one of the day's lectionary passages. Read the passage out loud.

b. Focus on this text without referring to other similar or contrasting passages: Who are the actors here? What happens?

c. Ask each participant to name something they notice in the text because of some aspect of their own identity or experience. (For example, "Because I am a mother, I notice . . . "; "Because I am a Canadian, I notice . . . "; "Because I feel like I have nothing to offer, I notice. . . .")

d. What new perspectives on the text do you gain as you listen to each other?

♦ Group *Lectio Divina* as Intervention (Appendix A, Part III, F)

Use the Square Dance Controversy from session 5 as a role-play. Find volunteers for the following parts. Provide each volunteer with a note describing their role. They will reveal the information gradually during the role-play.

Tim: You are a male in your late 40s, well respected in the congregation, and usually in some position of leadership. Currently you are chair of the congregation and are facilitating the meeting. Your sister, Ann, is part of the worship commission sub-committee that planned the dance. You are surprised by the level of concern, but ready to work with it.

Jen: You are a single woman in your late 20s and a very active member of the congregation. You live in the neighborhood and are interested in creative outreach to your neighbors.

Ann: You are a woman in your late 40s and a long-time member of worship commission. You are a sister to Tim, the chair of the congregation. You have been square dancing since high school, when most dancing was viewed with some suspicion by the church but such folk dancing was acceptable.

Dave: You are a married male in your mid 30s, with two young daughters. You are not part of the worship commission or the Sunday school class. You think square dancing is a healthy social activity and want your daughters to be part of a congregation where square dancing is acceptable.

Richard: You are in your early 70s and retired. When you were young, any form of dancing was considered sinful. Your own view has moderated over the years. You don't have a problem with people square dancing in other settings, but you wonder whether this is an appropriate church activity.

Ruth: You are in your mid 50s and well respected in the congregation, where you have often been in leadership roles, though you are not currently. You think the sign looks tacky and you wonder what people coming for the mission festival will think of it.

Joe: You are in your late 60s and retired. You were on the Church Council in the spring but your term has ended. You have a vague memory of the proposal but don't remember hearing about specifics like a dance, and certainly there was nothing about a portable sign.

Mark: You are the pastor, in your late 30s. You have been with the congregation for six years. You are an ex-officio part of the worship commission and are comfortable with the square dance. You see your role as hearing the concerns brought forward and helping the congregation to remember its commitment to direct address of conflict.

Tell the whole group the story of the Square Dance Controversy and then begin the role-play. Create two circles, with the volunteers doing the role-play in the center and others in the group watching from the outer circle. At a point when the discussion is intense and people seem stuck or unable to hear each other, intervene with the Group *Lectio Divina*, following the steps given in Appendix A. You may want to take the role of the pastor, and bring the intervention in his voice. You can use one of the following suggestions as the passage you read, or find one yourself that seems appropriate: Romans 13:8–10, Ephesians 4:1–6, Philippians 4:4–7, Colossians 3:14–16a.

After the intervention, continue the role-play, observing what change, if any, happens for the participants. At an appropriate moment, draw the role-play to a close. Spend some time as a larger group discussing what happened as a result of the intervention. Be sure to allow space for the role-play participants to speak to their experience of it. Discuss both what happened and how people felt about it.

SESSION 8

Prior to the session, read chapter 8 of *In Tune with God*: Discerning Next Steps.

Opening

Song suggestions: Gathering Chant; They that wait upon the Lord (*HWB* 584); or O Christe Domine Jesu (*HWB* 113)

Dialogue for Two Fools for Christ: Good-bye

Discussion and Practices

§ Group Discussion

- Do any of the personal barriers to discernment given in chapter 8 sound familiar?
- Does your congregation face any of the congregational barriers? How might you begin addressing such barriers?
- What helps you, or could help you, to be both realistic and expectant in thinking about congregational discernment?
- Is there anything from the congregational stories that inspires ideas for a next step that your own congregation might take?

- What ideas for a next step do you bring from other settings, such as another congregation, conflict transformation training, spiritual formation work, and so on?

☙ Group *Lectio Divina*

Spend time in a group *lectio divina* (as in session 3), or in attentive silence, opening yourself to God's love and being aware that deepening discernment is God's project, not our own. Suggested passages: Jeremiah 29:11, Revelation 22:17, Philippians 1:9–11, John 4:13–14.

☙ Discerning Next Steps

Brainstorm ideas for a next step that you could take in your own congregation. Record ideas on newsprint without evaluation.

a. Choose one or two to focus on by giving each participant three sticky dots and having them put one dot on each of their top three choices.

b. How can you strengthen or improve these ideas? What do you need in order to act on the idea(s)?

NOTE

[1] Norvene Vest, *Gathered in the Word*, 17–27.

One-day Retreat Outline

DEEPENING OUR CONGREGATIONAL DISCERNMENT

This retreat could be used to round out a group's work with the book, or could be used as a one-day event for participants who have read the book prior to the retreat.

Allow time for people to arrive and connect with each other. Begin with a time of worship (*30 minutes*). Continue to interweave song and attentive silence throughout the day.

Session One: Discovering current congregational discernment and decision making patterns (*1½ hours*)
1. As a group, respond to the question, "How do we make decisions now?" Record observations on newsprint and post these. It may help to focus on some recent decisions, looking at what the process was.
2. Look at your written bylaws or guidelines.
3. On your newsprint of observations, put a green asterisk beside elements that are in the written guidelines.
4. Consider the unmarked observations. Some of these will be your unwritten rules. Mark these with a blue asterisk.
5. Are there other unwritten rules you should note? Ask those who are relatively new to the congregation what they stumbled over, had to learn by observation, or have explained to them about your decision making.

Break

Session Two: Assessing current patterns (*1 hour*)
1. Re-gather with song or a time of attentive silence
2. Group discussion
    a. Which of your current practices strike you as having potential for growth and change?
    b. Which of your current practices strike you as problematic, or barriers to discernment?
    c. Which of your current practices do you affirm with enthusiasm?

Lunch

Session Three: Initial discerning (*1 hour*)
1. Present *Dialogue for Two Fools*—Good-bye
2. Re-gather with a group *lectio divina,* using one of the passages suggested in session 3 or 8, or one that you choose. (See Appendix A, Part III, F for the group *lectio divina* outline.)
3. Spend time in individual reflections, jotting down any nudges that came in the meditation, or other ideas you have had for an appropriate next step. Share these ideas in pairs, and then in the large group. Record the ideas on newsprint and post.

Break

Session Four: Discerning next steps (*1 hour*)
    Choose one or two possibilities to focus on by having each participant mark their top three choices with sticky dots. How can you strengthen or improve these ideas? What do you need in order to act on them?
    Close with a time of worship and thanks to God.

Bibliography

Avery, Michel, Brian Auvine, Barbara Streibel, and Lonnie Weiss. *Building United Judgment: A Handbook for Consensus Decision Making.* Madison, Wisconsin: Center for Conflict Resolution, 1981.

Bacon, Margaret Hope. "The Abolition of Slavery," in *The Quiet Rebels: The Story of the Quakers in America.* New York; London: Basic Books, Inc., 1969.

Bohler, Carolyn Stahl. *Opening to God: Guided Imagery Meditation on Scripture.* Nashville, Tennessee: Upper Room Books, 1996.

Drake, Thomas E. *Quakers and Slavery in America.* New Haven: Yale University Press, 1950.

Farnham, Suzanne G., Stephanie A. Hull, and R. Taylor McLean. *Grounded in God: Listening Hearts Discernment for Group Deliberations.* Harrisburg, Pennsylvania: Morehouse Publishing, 1999.

Farnham, Suzanne G., Joseph P. Gill, R. Taylor McLean, and Susan M. Ward. *Listening Hearts: Discerning Call in Community.* Harrisburg, Pennsylvania: Morehouse Publishing, 1991.

Fee, Gordon D. *Paul, the Spirit, and the People of God.* Peabody, Massachusetts: Hendrickson Publishers, 1996.

Fowl, Stephen E., and L. Gregory Jones. *Reading in Communion: Scripture and Ethics in Christian Life.* Grand Rapids, Michigan: Wm. B. Eerdmans Publishing, 1991.

Fretheim, Terrence E. *The Suffering of God: An Old Testament Perspective*. Philadelphia, Pennsylvania: Fortress Press, 1984.

Green, Thomas H., S.J. *Weeds among the Wheat: Discernment: Where Prayer and Action Meet*. Notre Dame, Indiana: Ave Maria Press, 1984.

Guder, Darrell L., et al. *Missional Church: A Vision for the Sending of the Church in North America*. Grand Rapids, Michigan: Wm. B. Eerdmans Publishing, 1998.

Hocker, Joyce L., and William W. Wilmot. *Interpersonal Conflict*, 4th ed. Madison, Wisconsin: Brown and Benchmark, 1995.

Johnson, Luke Timothy. *Scripture and Discernment: Decision making in the Church*. Nashville, Tennessee: Abingdon Press, 1983.

Kropf, Marlene. "Discerning God's Voice: Spiritual Discernment in Mennonite Congregations," in *Resource Packet for Congregational Discernment*. Elkhart, Indiana: Mennonite Board of Congregational Ministries, 1995.

LaCugna, Catharine Mowry. *God for Us: The Trinity and Christian Life*. San Francisco, California: HarperCollins Publishers, 1991.

Lamott, Anne. *Traveling Mercies: Some Thoughts on Faith*. New York, New York: Pantheon Books, 1999.

L'Engle, Madeleine. *A Wrinkle in Time*. New York, New York: Farrar, Strauss and Giroux, 1962.

Lederach, John Paul. *The Journey Toward Reconciliation*. Scottdale, Pennsylvania: Herald Press, 1999.

Lewis, C. S. *The Magician's Nephew*. Great Britain: The Bodley Head, 1955.

McKinney, Mary Benet, O.S.B. *Sharing Wisdom: A Process for Group Decision Making*. Allen, Texas: Tabor Publishing, 1987.

Morris, Danny E. and Charles M. Olsen. *Discerning God's Will Together: A Spiritual Practice for the Church*. Bethesda, Maryland: Alban Publications, 1997.

Mueller, Joan. *Faithful Listening: Discernment in Everyday Life*. Kansas City, Missouri: Sheed & Ward, 1996.

Mulholland, M. Robert, Jr. *Shaped by the Word: The Power of Scripture in Spiritual Formation*. Nashville, Tennessee: The Upper Room, 1985.

Olsen, Charles M. *Transforming Church Boards into Communities of Spiritual Leaders*. Bethesda, Maryland: The Alban Institute, 1995.

Oswald, Roy M., and Robert E. Friedrich Jr. *Discerning Your Congregation's Future*. Bethesda, Maryland: The Alban Institute, 1996.

Placher, William C. *Narrative of a Vulnerable God: Christ, Theology and Scripture*. Louisville, Kentucky: Westminster John Knox Press, 1994.

Purvis, Sally B. *The Power of the Cross: Foundations for a Christian Feminist Ethic of Community*. Nashville, Tennessee: Abingdon Press, 1993.

Schemel, George, S. J. and Sister Judith Roemer. "Communal Discernment," in *Review for Religious*, November–December 1981, 825–836.

Schertz, Mary, and Perry Yoder. *Seeing the Text: Exegesis for Students of Greek and Hebrew*. Nashville, Tennessee: Abingdon Press, 2001.

Schrock-Shenk, Carolyn, ed. *Mediation and Facilitation Training Manual: Foundations and Skills for Constructive Conflict Transformation*, 4th ed. Akron, Pennsylvania: Mennonite Conciliation Service, 2000.

Schrock-Shenk, Carolyn, and Lawrence Ressler. *Making Peace with Conflict: Practical Skills for Conflict Transformation*. Scottdale, Pennsylvania: Herald Press, 1999.

Sheeran, Michael J., S. J. *Beyond Majority Rule: Voteless Decisions in the Religious Society of Friends.* Philadelphia Yearly Meeting of the Religious Society of Friends, 1983.

Smucker, Marcus. "Facing Difficult Issues: Moral and Spiritual Discernment in Congregational decision making," in *Resource Packet for Congregational Discernment.* Elkhart, Indiana: Mennonite Board of Congregational Ministries, 1995.

Vest, Norvene. *Gathered in the Word: Praying the Scripture in Small Groups.* Nashville, Tennessee: Upper Room Books, 1996.

Wolff, Pierre. *Discernment: The Art of Choosing Well.* Liguori, Missouri: Triumph Books, 1993.

Yoder, John Howard. *Body Politics: Five Practices of the Christian Community before the Watching World.* Nashville, Tennessee: Discipleship Resources, 1997.